Vincennes University
Shake Learning Resources Center
Vincennes, Indiana 47591-9986

First Time Around
Case Studies of the Freshman Year Experience

Michael Welsh
University of South Carolina

KENDALL/HUNT PUBLISHING COMPANY
4050 Westmark Drive   Dubuque, Iowa 52002

Cover image courtesy of Corel.

Copyright © 1999 by Kendall/Hunt Publishing Company

ISBN 0-7872-6405-9

All rights reserved. No part of this publication may be reproduced, stored in a retrieval system, or transmitted, in any form or by any means, electronic, mechanical, photocopying, recording, or otherwise, without the prior written permission of the copyright owner.

Printed in the United States of America

10 9 8 7 6 5 4 3 2 1

Contents

Preface v

Introduction 1

Chapter 1   **Homesickness 5**
Rock Fever 7
Homesick in a Small Town 11
Hopeless 17

Chapter 2   **Parents 21**
Back Off 23
Let Go 27
Wish You Were Here 31

Chapter 3   **Old Friendships 35**
Home Sweet Home 37
Another Twist 41
Pulling Away 45

Chapter 4   **Making New Friends 49**
Designated Driver 51
The Eating Game 55
Late Night 59
Should I Leave? 63
The Lab Partner 67
Treat Me Like a Dummy 71
Just Five More Minutes 77

Chapter 5 **Professors and Staff 81**
Wounded Freshman 83
The Speech Instructor 87
On the Fringe 91
Speak English 95
The Flooded Room 99
Bureaucracy 103

Chapter 6 **Campus Safety 107**
Strange Glances 109
The Midnight Errand 113
The Stranger 117
Shaving Cream Initiations 121
The Chat Room 127

Chapter 7 **Academic Integrity 131**
When the Music Stops 133
Keeping the Scholarship 137
A Golden Opportunity 141
This Paper Is Plagiarized 145
Signing the Honor Code 153

Chapter 8 **Diversity 159**
Color Lines 161
Southern Hospitality 165

Preface

This casebook was born out of a desire to help instructors get to know their students. Teaching excellence requires nothing less. So, graduate assistants gaining practical teaching experience that included co-teaching a freshman seminar course at colleges in South Carolina including the University of South Carolina, Coker College, Newberry College, and Presbyterian College were encouraged to begin learning about their students by getting to know at least one freshman student in their class very well. This they accomplished by writing a case study about a problem or decision that one of their students faced in the first few weeks of college. Gathering the data for the case study brought the graduate students into close contact with at least one student whose family, social and educational background they learned in some detail and depth.

The graduate assistants were students in their second and final year of a master's degree program in student personnel services or higher education administration. They were each seeking to gain practical experience working with an experienced instructor in the University's renowned University 101 program to enhance career opportunities after graduation. They were selected for their interest in helping undergraduate students become successful in college and universities, their sensitivity to, and interest in, issues of diversity, their enthusiasm for the academic and co-curricular life in higher education institutions, and their willingness to model appropriate behaviors, like goal-setting and time management, for new students. The duties of these graduate students included attendance at all of their freshman seminar class meetings; planning the course content and syllabus; assisting with arranging visitors, speakers, and field trips; facilitating class discussions; serving as mentors for class members; providing student feedback to the instructor; and conducting class sessions as requested by the instructor.

The graduate students prepared the case studies contained in this book. And, emerging from their work and the freshmen they studied, it seems that the first great concern of traditional-aged college freshmen is personal relationships. The case studies show freshmen trying to work out new ways of relating to parents and family at home whom they have left behind; trying to figure out how they will continue their relationships with high-school friends who have scattered to other colleges and jobs; trying to learn how to maintain close relationships with boyfriends or girlfriends who may still be in high school or are attending another college; trying to adjust to living with new roommates and making new friends at college; and trying to find out how to deal with college professors and staff bureaucrats.

Negotiating this maze of relationships consumes more of the lives of freshmen in their first days of college than might be realized by college faculty and staff. If freshmen fail in working out their relationships, then they begin looking for and seeing the negative in their college experiences. If they are successful with their relationships, then a sense of security and confidence develops and students begin to realize that they can make it.

Hopefully, the case studies contained in this book will provide the kind of reality freshmen can relate to easily. The discussions based on the cases provide the opportunity for freshmen to "walk in the shoes" of their peers and to think through real-life problems. The result, it is hoped, will be for freshmen to become adept at resolving successfully for themselves the kinds of problems that so many freshmen face.

Introduction

The early weeks in college are when freshmen have their first time around with some of life's most interesting experiences. Much of it is exciting and exhilarating, yet some is frightful and uncertain. This is one time in life when almost all relationships in which a person is involved undergo change of one sort or another. High school friends go their separate ways and decisions have to be made about how to keep those friendships alive. Boyfriends and girlfriends are left behind. Promises of love are tested and parents missed. It's a crazy mix of happiness and sadness that washes over freshmen who suffer the loss of old friends and find the joy of new friends all in the same short time at the beginning of college.

This casebook contains the real-life stories of freshmen as they work through their problems in those first weeks of college. Each story is true. It describes a freshman faced with a decision or dilemma that really happened. The names of the students and their colleges have been changed for reasons of privacy, but the main facts of each case are true and accurate. These stories, or case studies as they are called, have been told to the authors of this book as a way of handing on to others the wisdom that new students have gained from their experiences in the first year of college.

The case studies were researched and written in cooperation with student affairs professionals who worked with new students in freshman seminar or orientation courses on a variety of campuses. Each case study has been carefully checked by the freshman whose case it was and, by means of a signed release form, verified as accurate and true. Care was taken at every step to ensure that nothing essential to the meaning of the case was "made up" and that each case study would ring true to freshmen on campuses across the country.

Sharing the Wisdom of Freshmen

Learning from case studies is best done in groups of freshmen where the dilemmas and problems contained in the cases are most keenly felt. Freshmen learn from the mistakes and problems of their peers. The knowledge gained from reading about, reflecting upon and discussing the real-life situations contained in these case studies is an early step for freshmen in coming to the wisdom needed for successfully negotiating the perilous trail to a college degree.

The advantage of using case studies is that they bypass the awkwardness many freshmen feel talking about their own personal issues in a freshman seminar or college success class. Instead, they can work through cases and, in the process, can practice and sharpen the skills needed to solve their own issues and succeed in college. Those would include skills in critical thinking, problem solving, effective written and oral communication, and leadership.

Solving Cases

The actual benefit of solving cases comes from placing yourself in the position of the freshman in the case study who must take a stand and resolve an issue. You cannot be a spectator or outside observer. You must take on the role and responsibilities of the main character in the case together with the surrounding facts, opinions, and prejudices upon which that character had to depend at the time the case was actually unfolding. This allows you to develop and exercise your own skills and judgment on real-life problems.

Case learning is a "safe" way to learn how to deal with some awkward and difficult problems. Safe in the sense that no one will be hurt if you happen to make a mistake in coming to what you judge to be the best solution for the case. Case learning gives you the opportunity to experience through the eyes of real freshmen the kinds of problems you may well confront in your own life as a new college student.

Preparing for a Case Discussion

Many freshmen will be encountering case studies for the first time. To help you prepare for a case discussion, a **Case Analysis Worksheet** is provided at the end of each case. This worksheet helps you identify the key facts in the case, the problems or issues that need to be resolved, alternative solutions that might be used, and what you would consider to be the best solution for the case and why you think it is best. Basically, the worksheet follows a four-step critical thinking process:

1. Determine what the case is about and what facts are most important;

2. Identify the problems, issues, or questions that need to be resolved;

3. List a number of solutions that might be used to solve the case;

4. Determine the best solution.

Before using the worksheet, you should quickly read or scan the case study to get some idea of what the case is about. Many times, you can do that by just by reading the first paragraph and the last paragraph. These two paragraphs often contain a snapshot of the problem in the case. The paragraphs in between are filled with facts and details that round out the full story. They give you the information you need to immerse yourself in the case and "become" the person whose role and responsibility are the subject of the case. Once you inhabit the situation and face the problem as your own, you can begin to analyze the case using your own skills, talents, background and biases.

Case Discussion

After you have completed your individual preparation by carefully reading the case, reflecting upon what you would do in the same situation and completing the case analysis worksheet, then you are ready to discuss the case with your classmates. Most likely your instructor will assign you to a small group to discuss the case, after which the whole class will come together to again discuss the case.

The small group discussion is important because it gives you an opportunity to test your individual preparation and to teach others in the group what you know about the case. If you can communicate what you have learned about a case so that others understand what you are talking about, then you also know.

The discussion will work best if you and your group agree to follow some very basic rules. These rules were first used by the ancient philosopher, Socrates, to maintain a sense of collegiality as he and his contemporaries debated various issues.

- Establish dialogue. "Dialogue" means "talking through" and the key to dialogue is to exchange ideas without trying to change other people's minds.

- Exchange ideas. This gives you the opportunity to compare your own ideas against those of others.

- Don't argue.

- Don't interrupt.

- Listen carefully. Focus entirely upon whoever is speaking. This is difficult at first. It sounds easy, but it takes practice.

- Clarify your thinking. To do this, you must first suspend all untested assumptions. Check your assumptions about everything and try to maintain an unbiased view.

- Be honest. Say what you think, even if your thoughts are controversial. Once people believe they know what you really think, they will usually be more comfortable and open around you.

(These rules were adapted from: Michiko, M. (1993). "Einstein's teamwork secret." *Training*. 60-61.)

These same rules apply to the large group or class discussion. In this discussion the class as a whole has the chance to push the quality and quantity of learning beyond the individual and small group stages. It is in this discussion that you can reach a thorough understanding of the case and an optimal resolution of the issue or problem. The collective efforts of all your classmates aided by your instructor provides the chance to lift your learning to higher levels.

Note to Instructors

Freshmen demand relevance from classes and may have little patience or attention span for classroom lectures. They do not feel they need some adult telling them about their problems. The lecture method teaches students to expect the instructor to provide the right answers. Case teaching, on the other hand, involves facilitating a dialogue where many answers are possible but none of them is perfect. There are "better solutions" and "worse solutions," but never a "right answer."

Explaining or "lecturing" a case to students does not use the power of the case method of instruction to best advantage. The power is in allowing students to test their own best solutions against the wisdom of their classmates in a process of dialog and discussion. Most of us have learned by traditional lecture methods and we tend to teach like we were taught. Teaching by the case method seems a bit mysterious and some of us just do not have the time to learn a new method of instruction. But, it is worth it to see the valuable learning and excitement that freshmen experience when they solve problems that bear directly on their own lives.

You can learn more about the case method of instruction from these selected writings:

Christensen, C.R. (1987). *Teaching and the Case Method.* Boston: Harvard Business School Publishing Division.

Christensen, C. R., Garvin, D. A, & Sweet, A. (1991). *Education for Judgment: The Artistry of Discussion Leadership.* Boston: Harvard Business School.

Erskine, J. A., Leenders, M. R., & Mauffette-Leenders, L. A. (1998). *Teaching with Cases.* London, Ontario, Canada: Richard Ivey School of Business.

Gragg, C. (1954). Because wisdom can't be told. In M. McNair (Ed.), *The Case Method at Harvard Business School*, (pp. 6-14). New York: McGraw-Hill Book Company, Inc.

Mauffette-Leenders, L. A., Erskine, J. A., & Lenders, M. R. (1997). *Learning with Cases.* London, Ontario, Canada: Richard Ivey School of Business.

Welty, W. (1989). Discussion method teaching: How to make it work. *Change, 21,* 40-49.

CHAPTER 1

Homesickness

It is a rare person who does not feel at a loss when away from the familiar sights and sounds of home. Sometimes it hurts very much not to be able to go home and feel the security that we find there.

Homesickness generally refers to feelings of sadness, loss of meaning, fearing change, anticipating disappointment, or loneliness. It can affect any of us when we move to new places and have to meet our needs with different people and in new ways.

There is no magic cure. It does help, however, to talk to someone when you experience sadness. Often others can show us how to make new meanings for ourselves and can help us resolve our sadness by allowing us to face our feelings and come to new self understanding.

■ Rock Fever

Axel Larson felt alone and isolated during the first few weeks at college. He had left his home in Hawaii to study at a college on the East coast. He felt out of place among his fellow students and wondered if he had made a big mistake in coming this far to college.

■ Homesick in a Small Town

As she approached her third week away from home, Elise McKinna was overpowered by her feelings of homesickness. She had come all the way from Texas to play soccer on scholarship at a small rural college in South Carolina. She began feeling sadness the day after she arrived, and it only got worse as the days went by. She missed her family and boyfriend and was disappointed with her new soccer team. "What have I done to myself," she wondered.

■ Hopeless _____

Her residence hall was quiet again this weekend and Caroline Whyte felt very lonely. Her roommate had a boyfriend with whom she spent most of her time and everyone else seemed to leave each weekend. Fall break was just around the corner and Caroline wanted to take that opportunity to go home and not come back.

Suggested Readings

Holkeboer, R. (1996). *Right for the Start: Managing Your College Career.* Belmont, CA: Wadsworth Publishing Company. Chapter 2.

Newman, B. M. & Newman, P. R. (1996). "Loneliness." In Gordon, V. N. & Minnick (Eds.) *Foundations: A Reader for New College Students.* Belmont, CA: Wadsworth Publishing Company. 61-62.

CASE STUDY

Rock Fever

(This case study was prepared in cooperation with Sarah Huntington, Resident Director and Coordinator of Student Activities, at Sonoma State University. It is intended solely to initiate class discussion. All names and some peripheral facts have been disguised.)

Axel Hercules Larson found himself isolated and alone during those first few weeks of college. He came all the way to the East coast from his home in Hawaii to study marine biology. Now, he wondered if it was all a big mistake.

Axel's parents and older sister moved to Hawaii when he was four years old. He lived his whole life there, leaving only once to visit Washington, D.C. As a child, the beach was his only playground. Surfing easily became his passion and he prided himself on his ability to ride the really big waves. Jazz was important too. He was part of a small three-piece jazz band that was beginning to get gigs in places all around the island. Many of his friends did not understand why he decided to leave all of this to go to college. More, why he would go to a college so far away was even more of a mystery to them. He was the only one in his high school graduating class who decided to go on to college. Axel had tired of the island. He had gotten "rock fever" as they say; like cabin fever, it made you just want to get out. "I had gotten as much as possible out of Hawaii, I had to move on," was the way Axel put it.

At seventeen, Axel was one of the younger college freshmen. Good looking, with long brown curly hair worn in a ponytail and blue eyes, he wore the long, loose-fitting shorts and shirts of the laid-back surf culture. His name was different and stood out—he liked that. Around his neck was a wooden bead necklace strung on a leather lace and on his feet black sneakers.

He felt out of place on a campus where everybody wore jeans and T-shirts and carried backpacks. People asked, "Where are you from? You're not from around here," and he thought he must stick out like a sore thumb.

Axel thought his new university might be too fast-paced and set in its ways. "People are already into their cliques," he lamented. He missed the diversity of Hawaii's people and landscape. He had chosen the university because his grandmother lived in a small town about 25 miles from campus. Staying with her had made it affordable for him to leave Hawaii to attend college. Luckily, his grandmother had a neighbor who worked near the university and did not mind having Axel ride back and forth each day. That meant he did not have to buy a car, which he didn't think he could afford anyway.

"Looking back," he had written in his journal, "I wish I'd signed up to live on campus to find my niche, but it was too expensive." He even began to regret leaving Hawaii as he wrote, "It figures . . . just when I was getting ready to leave the island, things began to look up. My jazz group was getting gigs; I was working on the set of Waterworld, and I even met a girl."

Now he was not so sure he had made the right decision to come this far to study. The doubt nagged him and he wondered what he should do. "If I've made a mistake, I want to correct it," he thought to himself.

Name _____ Date _____

CASE ANALYSIS WORKSHEET

Rock Fever

What is this case about? Immerse yourself in the case by putting yourself in Axel Larson's position. When you do, you will see yourself as a freshman with an unusual name that has come all the way from Hawaii to the East coast to attend college. You feel isolated and alone. And you begin wondering if you might have made a mistake.

Get the facts. List the facts that you know about Axel Larson and the situation:

1. _____
2. _____
3. _____
4. _____
5. _____

State the problem, issue or question that needs to be resolved.

_____
_____

List several ways that the problem might be resolved.

1. _____
2. _____
3. _____

Write down the best way to solve the problem and why you would solve it that way.

_____
_____
_____

CASE STUDY

Homesick in a Small Town

(This case study was prepared in cooperation with Sean Lehlbach, Graduate Assistant at the University of South Carolina. It is intended solely to initiate class discussion. All names and some peripheral facts have been disguised.)

The town was too small; there were only 300 students in the college; and the women's soccer team was no better than recreational level. That was what Elise McKinna found when she traveled from her home in the Dallas-Ft. Worth area to rural South Carolina to play soccer on a scholarship. Worse, her feelings of homesickness seemed to overpower everything as she approached her third week away from home.

"What have I done to myself?" she wondered silently as she picked up the phone to call home.

Her Soccer Scholarship

Elise played on a high school soccer team that was one of the most respected in Texas. Many of her teammates were recruited to play at the large Division I universities in Texas. But, Elise's small 5'4" frame did not impress coaches at the big schools and she had accepted a scholarship at Moore College in Reevesville, South Carolina. She wanted to become more independent and to play soccer at the collegiate level. Moving to South Carolina forced her to learn to be independent of her family because it took her so far away from them. About the soccer, however, she was not so sure.

From her very first soccer practice, Elise tried to play hard. But, it was a battle. She learned quickly that the team did not follow training rules very strictly and did not seem to care about the soccer skills and knowledge that Elise brought from the winning teams she played with in Texas. Her first impressions of the Moore College team was that it was more suited for recreational soccer than for competition at the collegiate level.

After the first several days of soccer practice, Elise saw the team begin to come around. She made the starting line up and actually began looking forward to the first game. A lesson she learned in those first days on the soccer field was that she could be a better leader by actions rather than by words. The coach also seemed to be doing a good job with the players and they were starting to gel as a team. Elise could not wait to score her first college goal and to feel the excitement and joy of winning her first college game.

A week and a half later the team played its first game of the season. It was an away game and they lost 5-0. Elise felt that she played well, but she got sick during the game. Being sick really made her want to be home with her mom.

Two days later, they played their first home game. Elise scored two goals and had three assists in a 10-0 win. She was tired from being sick, but still played well. She was the only freshman on the starting team, and yet, she did not feel she had found her "groove" with the team. They just did not play her style of soccer, so she felt she had to struggle to fit into the system. She thought about the soccer offer she still had from a small college back in Texas. If she took it she could be close to her family and her boyfriend. Plus, she could get her own apartment and play on a team with a couple of her old teammates and good friends. It was a tempting thought.

Her Family

Elise wanted to learn to be independent. On her fourth day at Moore College she wrote in her journal:

> *So far I have learned that Moore seems to bring in nothing but nice people. Everyone here has been so friendly and more adult-like. I dealt with a lot of immature people and it has been so great to come here and be around mature people. I've only been here since Saturday, so I haven't quite seen it all. I have come to really like my roommate. She has a lot of the same interests and I love to hear all her stories about her life. My first day of classes, I learned that my professors all seem to want the same things as I do. That is to learn and have a good time doing it. With the exception of one, but I'll deal with that somehow.*

Soon Elise realized that she was away from home and would not be able to see her family for awhile. Hers was a close-knit family, one she described as being a "Beaver Cleaver family." Both sets of grandparents lived in the same town as did all three of her older brothers. Already she missed sitting around with all of them during their frequent family gatherings. Her parents were laid back and their home was always the center of activity. With five children, the house was always filled with the kids and their friends. It was the kind of place where kids were welcomed and felt comfortable hanging out there.

On Sunday, after her first week away, she talked to her little brother on the phone. He really missed her and she missed him. She just wanted to fly home and give him a big hug and kiss. Instead, she wrote him letters telling him how she felt. She found writing a good way to deal with her feelings, calling was just too expensive. The following Saturday was his birthday and this would be the first time that she had not been home to celebrate with him. She bought him a Moore College T-shirt so he could always remember where she was. The thought made her sad, and also reminded her of how lonely she was for her boyfriend. She hoped he still remembered where she was.

Her Boyfriend

The hardest part about leaving Texas was that Elsie would be a long way from her boyfriend, Scott. She and Scott had been dating for seven months. This was her first long relationship and Scott meant more to her than anyone she had ever dated because he was a respectful person who liked her for who she was and did not try to change her. As she saw it, they were a serious couple.

Scott had remained in Texas to play college football on a scholarship. He was a starting linebacker as a freshman and Elise wished she could be there for his first game. It was on the same day as her younger brother's birthday and she found herself doubly upset that she could not be there for either event. She was saddened to think that she might not be able to see any of Scott's games during his first season.

Elise missed Scott more than anyone. A day never passed that she did not think of him. He called every week and, during her second week away, he said he was going to try to come and see her during the next weekend. The thought of him coming to see her really lifted her spirits. If he came, he would be there for her first home game, and she loved it when he watched her play. He gave her great confidence in herself. Just the anticipation that he might come to South Carolina brightened her days and took her mind off her bout with homesickness.

Homesickness

As soon as Elise realized that she was no longer in Texas and would not get to see her family or Scott for a long time, she began feeling the pangs of homesickness. It flared up the second day after she arrived at Moore College. She had chosen to move far away from home, not because she wanted to get away from an unhappy home life, but because she wanted to learn independence. She was the only girl among four brothers and she wanted to do something that none of her older brothers had done, namely, go to college far from home.

After a week, Elise was still uncomfortable at Moore College. The soccer team was not what she had thought it would be and her recruiting visit to the campus last Spring had not prepared her for the smallness of both the campus and the town of Reevesville. Her home in Texas was close to centers of activity that included the Texas Rangers, Dallas Cowboys, Six Flags Over Texas, a waterpark, and a huge mall. Everything was right there. In Reevesville, on the other hand, she could walk to almost anyplace in town in just a few minutes, but there wasn't much there. They did not have a mall, not even a small one. It was like the small Texas town where her aunt and uncle lived. She remembered how boring it was to visit them.

Every morning Elise woke up with a feeling of homesickness. She learned that life is just not the same when you are on your own. But she was determined to deal with those feelings and tried to keep her spirits high. On some days she was crippled by homesickness, but on other days she was only lightly touched. When Scott called and said he might come to visit, her days became much brighter. "Even if he doesn't come," she reasoned, "at least there will be a day or two when I'm not so homesick."

At the end of her second week on campus, Elise was still "fighting the good fight" against homesickness. In her journal she wrote:

> *This is a really serious issue with me and I'm afraid my homesickness will start to affect me, but not grades or soccer wise. I'm so confused and somewhat feel alone, but I'm just trying to keep my spirits high. It is working pretty good so far.*

By the end of her third week things seemed to have gotten worse. She and Scott had decided not to call each other for two to three weeks. They both knew it would be hard, but she knew they had to stick it out. Scott had not been able to come see her play in the first home game. But, after the game she went out and had some fun. As soon as she returned to her room, she wanted to go home again. College just was not what she had expected it to be. "If you don't drink, there really is no one to hang out with, and those who don't drink get on my nerves" she thought to herself. "I just don't fit into a small town environment."

On Sunday, just three weeks after she arrived at college, she woke up more homesick than ever. She felt she could not take another day of homesick feelings and sadness. "I don't fit in out here," she concluded. "I can't find anyone like me. It's like there's no variety at this school. You either drink or hang out with people you can't stand. No one meshes with my personality."

Last week Elise had failed her first English paper. She had always gotten As and was upset and embarrassed with the failing grade. She had worked hard on the paper and thought she had done a good job. What a disappointment. She felt helpless and just wanted to go home.

"What have I done to myself?" Elise wondered as she reached for the phone to call her parents.

Name _____ Date _____

CASE ANALYSIS WORKSHEET

Homesick in a Small Town

What is this case about? Immerse yourself in this case by imagining yourself in Elise McKinna's position. You have come all the way from Texas to play soccer on scholarship at a small rural college in South Carolina. You felt sadness the day after you arrived and it has only gotten worse as the days pass. You miss your family and boyfriend and are disappointed in your soccer team.

Get the facts. List the facts that you know about Elise McKinna and the situation:

1. _____

2. _____

3. _____

4. _____

5. _____

State the problem, issue or question that needs to be resolved.

_____

_____

List several ways that the problem might be resolved.

1. _____

2. _____

3. _____

Write down the best way to solve the problem and why you would solve it that way.

_____

_____

CASE STUDY

Hopeless

(This case study was prepared in cooperation with David Clurman, Housing Director, Pennsylvania State University, and Amy Leahy, Assistant Director of Career Planning, Clemson University. It is intended solely to initiate class discussion. All names and some peripheral facts have been disguised.)

Caroline Whyte looked out the window of her room and sighed heavily. It was quiet in her hall again this weekend, and she felt lonely. Her roommate was over at her boyfriend's place *again*. So far she was not happy at college and was thinking about calling it quits. "I don't like it here," she thought, "what's the point of staying?"

Hampton University was a long way from home. Caroline had expected it to be a little more familiar to her than it turned out to be. She had lived here once when she was five years old. Even though her family had lived in the Midwest for most of her life, Caroline wanted to come to school in the south for the university's sports administration program, and to "be different."

When she was registering for classes, Caroline's advisor recommended that she not take University 101, which was a course that helped freshmen students adjust to college. Almost all students at Hampton University take the class and everyone seems to think that it does help them. In the classes that she was taking, Caroline was doing pretty well. Her grades were mostly Bs so far. Caroline wondered if taking University 101 might have been a good idea.

Even though she was shy, Caroline got very involved in high school. College was a different story. She joined the sports administration club as soon as she was settled on campus; but she still did not feel like she was a part of things. Her roommate spent most of her time with her boyfriend. As she thought about it, she got more frustrated. "Why does everyone on my floor have to leave town every weekend?" It was hard to get to know people when they never seemed to be around. "It's not like my RA is ever here, either," she thought.

Caroline started calling her parents and her boyfriend every day and told them how much she disliked school. Her calls became so frequent that her mother called the hall director where Caroline lived to see if he might be able to help her get over her homesickness. There was a small light at the end of the tunnel: the four-day fall break was coming up and Caroline could not wait to go home. She wanted to go home and not come back, but her mother said that she should try to stick it out for the rest of the semester. Her dad wanted her to stay for the rest of the year, but the thought of that depressed her. Her dad thought that she just needed time to adjust. Caroline knew that she would hate it more each day.

Caroline did not want to be a disappointment to her parents, but she really wanted to leave school and not come back. She thought about what she could have done to make things better, but it seemed hopeless.

Name _____ Date _____

CASE ANALYSIS WORKSHEET

Hopeless

What is this case about? Immerse yourself in this case by putting yourself in Caroline Whyte's shoes. Feel the loneliness of the weekend when her roommate was away visiting her boyfriend and everyone else had left campus for the weekend. Fall break is not far off and you just want to go home and not come back.

Get the facts. List the facts that you know about Caroline and the situation:

1. _____
2. _____
3. _____
4. _____
5. _____

State the problem, issue or question that needs to be resolved.

_____
_____

List several ways that the problem might be resolved.

1. _____
2. _____
3. _____

Write down the best way to solve the problem and why you would solve it that way.

_____
_____
_____

Parents

How to relate with parents after you have moved away for college can be difficult for new college students and for parents. Some of you may feel like you are prisoners of your parents' dreams and others may realize that when you return home, you will no longer be a child. Both can make you sad.

However, college is a time for young men and women to develop their independence. Parents' calls checking on freshmen are usually welcomed because they show that someone cares when the isolation and loneliness of college is most intense; but calling every morning and every evening to see how the day went probably does not foster that independence.

■ Back Off

Kevin's parents called every day and even dropped by his dorm room unannounced. Kevin Cosgrove loved them and needed them. He had been blind since he was ten and his parents tended to overprotect him; but now that he was in college he wanted some independence and wondered how he could make his parents understand that.

■ Let Go

Lynette DeMarco's mother called her two and sometimes three times a day to see if everything was okay. Her mother seemed to imagine the worst and her daily questioning frustrated Lynette. She wondered how she might convince her parents that she could take care of herself.

■ Wish You Were Here

A young freshman, Ruth Swenson, was happy at college and adjusted very well to her new surroundings. Her mother, however, had not adjusted to having her daughter away and called often asking her to come home for a weekend visit. Feeling guilty, Ruth went home for a weekend in October, but by Saturday afternoon was ready to return to college.

Suggesting Reading

Colburn, K. L., & Treeger, M. L. (1997). *Letting Go: A Parent's Guide to Understanding the College Years*. New York: Harper-Collins Publishers.

CASE STUDY

Back Off

(This case study was prepared in cooperation with Jeffrey M. Colburn, Assistant Director of Clubs, Georgia Tech Alumni Association, Georgia Tech University. It is intended solely to initiate class discussion. All names and some peripheral facts have been disguised.)

Kevin Cosgrove felt he had successfully made the transition to college. His parents had not; at least that was the way it seemed to Kevin. They called every day and even dropped by his dorm room unannounced a couple of times. "I love them and need them," he told his suitemate, "but they need to back off."

Kevin was a freshman at Southern University, a large urban university of 26,000 students. Blind since childhood, he had lived in the shadow of the university his whole life. His family's home was just across the river about a mile from the campus. He, his parents and older sister had lived the life of a typical American family.

Growing up, Kevin experienced the same things that most middle class kids experienced. He was involved in karate since he was five and was a brown belt by the time he entered college. He liked to ride his bike around the neighborhood with his friends. At the age of ten, however, he fell off his bike and fractured his skull. He recovered, but never forgot that accident.

Helping his dad had been something Kevin always enjoyed. He liked it when they puttered around the house or worked on the car. He learned a lot that way; simply doing things. He was mechanically inclined for as long as he could remember. That inclination led to some situations characteristic of childhood. "I was a holy terror growing up," he remembered. "I was always getting into things." He had a natural curiosity about everything.

When Kevin was eleven, his sister got a computer. The novelty of it soon wore off, and the computer did little more than sit in the living room. No one touched it. Kevin decided one day to check it out. He learned all about that computer, mostly from hands-on learning. When his sister went away to college, the computer stayed home. Kevin continued to learn more about computers through trial and error and learning what he could from manuals. He really enjoyed working with that computer. He was never afraid to experiment.

Kevin did well in high school. He scored As and Bs in all of his classes during his four years. When it came time to apply to colleges, Kevin knew where he wanted to go. His sister had gone to a small college about an hour's drive from home. But, Kevin was going to stay in town. He wanted to go to Southern University and experience all that the large school had to offer. He also knew that he wanted to major in computer science. He applied to and was accepted by the College of Science and Mathematics at Southern University.

He attended the orientation program offered by the university in June prior to his freshman year. The campus was big. Even though he had lived in the area all his life, he was not familiar with much of the campus. He did not know if his residence hall would be in a convenient location, or how he would find all of his classrooms, or even where he would eat.

When Kevin moved into his residence hall in August, he met his roommate. They got along OK, but his roommate had requested a private room and when one became available, he moved. So, Kevin was left without a roommate. However, he did share a bathroom with another student who was confined to a wheelchair. They quickly became good friends and kind of considered each other as roommates even though they each had the privacy of their own rooms.

Kevin wanted to live on campus so he could gain some independence from his parents. Attending Southern was Kevin's idea, but attending college was his parents' decision. They always wanted the best for him. He knew that and had no desire to "get away" from them; but he wondered if they might be crowding him a bit too much. His blindness had, perhaps, given them reason to be a little overprotective, but the calls and visits were more than he thought were needed. He wanted them to back off and wondered how he could make that happen.

Name _____ Date _____

CASE ANALYSIS WORKSHEET

Back Off

What is this case about?   Put yourself in Kevin Cosgrove's place and imagine your parents calling you every day and sometimes dropping by your dorm room unannounced. You are blind and you love your parents and need them, but now that you are in college you want to do things on your own. How do you make your parents understand that?

Get the facts.   List the facts that you know about Kevin and his situation:

1. _____

2. _____

3. _____

4. _____

5. _____

State the problem, issue or question that needs to be resolved.

_____

_____

List several ways that the problem might be resolved.

1. _____

2. _____

3. _____

Write down the best way to solve the problem and why you would solve it that way.

_____

_____

_____

CASE STUDY

Let Go

(This case study was prepared in cooperation with Donna Deragon, Graduate Assistant at the University of South Carolina. It is intended solely to initiate class discussion. All names and some peripheral facts have been disguised.)

Another phone call from Mom. "Where were you?" "What time did you get in?" "Who were you with?" Lynette hung up the phone after another uneasy conversation with her mother. "When will she just let go?" she wondered aloud in the quiet of her apartment.

Lynette DeMarco had been a freshman at the university only a few weeks, but things had settled down and she had developed a routine with which she was mostly comfortable. She lived about 10 minutes from campus in a one-bedroom apartment that she really liked because it was quiet and she could study without distractions. Its only drawback was that it made it difficult to meet people.

Lynette grew up in Cape May, New Jersey—the oldest resort town in the country. That was where her parents still lived after 25 years of marriage, and most of her relatives also lived close by. Her brother currently attended Slippery Rock University, but everyone else stayed pretty close to home. She never really understood why exactly, because her's was not a close family. She had even said to Laura, her best friend, "I'm uncomfortable around family, you can't talk with them like you can your friends. They're typical Northeasterners; never open with hugs and kisses."

Academic success was very important to Lynette. She studied diligently in high school and graduated valedictorian in a class of 250. Her SAT score was 1400 and with it she applied to some of the top colleges along the East coast, including Yale, Princeton, Boston University, Lafayette, University of Richmond, and University of South Carolina. With the exception of Princeton, she was accepted by all the colleges to which she applied. She chose the University of South Carolina because it was the farthest from home and had a highly respected international studies program.

Laura Heffler was Lynette's closest friend in high school. Their boyfriends were brothers, and the four of them hung out constantly together for the last two years, horseback riding and taking their mountain bikes for long day-trips into the hills around Cape May. Laura planned to move to South Carolina and share the apartment with Lynette while attending the community college there. But, a few weeks before the move, Laura was offered a modeling contract and a chance to audition on Broadway. She just could not turn it down, so she decided not to go to South Carolina.

Lynette's boyfriend had decided to attend the University of California at Santa Cruz. Because they would be separated by such a great distance, they decided that they could each date other people. That way they would learn for sure if they were meant to be with each other.

Moving to South Carolina was not as easy as Lynette had thought it would be. For the two weeks before she was to leave, her mother seemed to argue with her over everything. The arguments were over little things, but it was frustrating for Lynette. She heard lectures about locking doors and always having mace with her. Her parents were still upset about how Laura had left Lynette with the apartment lease. To Lynette, it seemed more time was spent reassuring everyone that she could take care of herself than was actually spent packing her things for the move.

Her parents and her grandmother drove her to South Carolina.

Emotions ran high when the time finally came for them to leave Lynette behind in her apartment and begin the return trip home. She could not believe it when she saw her mother, grandmother, and even her dad cry as they said good-bye. The scene was overwhelming. When the door shut and she found herself alone, she thought, "Wow, I'm here. Now, what do I do?"

She did not have long to wait. Her mom called her three times during the drive back to New Jersey. "Was she alright?" "Did she have everything she needed?"

For the next two weeks, Lynette's mom called her two or three times a day. Naturally, she was not always home when her mom called, and when that occurred she would later be drilled with questions; "Where were you? What time did you get in? Who were you with?" Her mother even called her at 8 a.m. on Saturday morning!

The calling and checking up on her frustrated Lynette. Her mother's habit of imagining the worst was unsettling. Today, as she hung up the phone, she wondered aloud, "What can I do to prove to my parents (and to myself) that I am going to be okay?"

Name _____ Date _____

CASE ANALYSIS WORKSHEET

Let Go

What is this case about? Immerse yourself in this case by imagining that you are Lynette DeMarco and your mother calls two or three times a day. You want to convince your mother that you can take care of yourself.

Get the facts. List the facts that you know about Lynette and her situation:

1. _____
2. _____
3. _____
4. _____
5. _____

State the problem, issue or question that needs to be resolved.

_____
_____

List several ways that the problem might be resolved.

1. _____
2. _____
3. _____

Write down the best way to solve the problem and why you would solve it that way.

_____
_____
_____
_____

CASE STUDY

Wish You Were Here

(This case study was prepared in cooperation with Michael P. Shuman, Academic Coordinator and Coordinator of Special Services, Wake Forest University. It is intended solely to initiate class discussion. All names and some peripheral facts have been disguised.)

Ruth Swenson had given in. She had finally gone home to visit. Everything looked about the same. The street had new paving and her dad had done a little redecorating, but nothing much had changed. She could not help but think about how much she would love to get back to school. She had only been home for one day, but she wanted to say good-bye and get back to life at college.

Ruth was a freshman in her first semester at Clickman College. She had developed a great circle of friends and was pleased with her grades and progress in school so far. Unfortunately, she could not help but feel guilty about not spending time at home in Anderson, a small town about an hour and a half away from the college. She loved her mother; at times she even considered her mom to be her very best friend. But, Ruth had grown tired of having the same conversation with her every time she called, which had become about three times a week.

"Ruth, why don't you ever come home for a visit? You dad works every night anymore and you know how your brother is. . . . I really miss not having you around. Why don't you come home, we're only an hour and a half away?"

Ruth always gave the same reply, "Mom . . . Mom . . . stop making me feel so guilty! I'd love to come home but I'm *really* busy this week. I have a paper due on Tuesday and I have plans to go to the game with some friends from my hall on Saturday. Besides, I'll be home for Thanksgiving next month."

"Oh . . . I know. I understand," she sighed. "I went away to college and left my folks at home way back when. It's alright."

"Okay then. So what else is new . . ."

"But," her mom interrupted, "I get so lonely and I was just thinking about how nice it would be to have you come home for a visit."

These conversations always made Ruth feel so guilty. Why did her mom always have to say, "I miss you" and "I'm lonely?" Every time Ruth was having fun or was about to go out on a Friday night with her friends, she couldn't help but think of her mom sitting at home all alone wishing her only daughter would come home to visit. She thought to herself, "Why can't Mom realize that I have a life here at Clickman?"

Her brother, Eric, was also away at college but too busy to visit with Mom. Plus, he did not have the same relationship with their mother that Ruth had. She knew her father was around sometimes, but he worked a lot and Ruth did not have much to say to him anyway. She knew he loved her, and that was enough.

On the third weekend in October, Ruth finally gave in and drove home Friday afternoon intending to stay until Sunday. On Saturday afternoon she realized how much she really wanted to be at Clickman. "How can I say good-bye," she wondered.

Name _____ Date _____

CASE ANALYSIS WORKSHEET

Wish You Were Here

What is this case about?   Put yourself in Ruth Swenson's shoes. Your mother misses you and wants you to come home and visit. You do, but after a day you're ready to return to college.

Get the facts.   List the facts that you know about Ruth and her situation:

1. _____

2. _____

3. _____

4. _____

5. _____

State the problem, issue or question that needs to be resolved.

_____

_____

List several ways that the problem might be resolved.

1. _____

2. _____

3. _____

Write down the best way to solve the problem and why you would solve it that way.

_____

_____

_____

_____

CHAPTER 3

Old Friendships

High school friendships begin to slip away as distance and the many changes demanded by college life reduce a person's availability for maintaining and nurturing these friendships. However, real friendships are not easily abandoned. Friendships formed in high school can last a lifetime, giving us one of life's most precious and valued experiences. Among the many adjustments to college is figuring out how to hang on to these friendships and keep them from fading away during the college years.

■ Home Sweet Home

Trey Johnson had not wanted to leave his family and girlfriend behind when he left for a distant university in another state. At first he was homesick, but soon he became involved in the party scene. During his first semester the girlfriend he left behind said she only wanted to be "just friends"; his parents announced that they were getting a divorce; and three of his high school friends were seriously injured in an auto accident. As the Christmas holidays approached, he wondered if he wanted to go home.

■ Another Twist

LaTonya Jones is trying to maintain a relationship with her boyfriend from high school. Theirs is an interracial relationship of which his parents do not approve. He is completely dependent upon his parents since he was paralyzed in an auto accident in his senior year and lives at home. She is now in college and the added pressures lead her to question whether she can continue in the relationship.

■ Pulling Away

Going away to college meant leaving behind his girlfriend to finish her senior year of high school. Richard Lukas was reluctant to leave Tina Miranda behind, but consoled himself by the thought that he would spend most weekends back home. After two weeks, Tina told Richard that she wanted to break up, but remain friends. Richard was hurt and wanted to end the relationship. He wondered how he might do so.

Suggested Reading

Chichton, Jennifer. "College friends." In Chaffee, John. (1995). *The Thinker's Guide to College Success*. Boston: Houghton Mifflin Company. 150-153.

CASE STUDY

Home Sweet Home

(This case study was prepared in cooperation with Carie Warnock, Coordinator of Research and Project Development, University of South Carolina. It is intended solely to initiate class discussion. All names and some peripheral facts have been disguised.)

Trey Johnson had not wanted to leave home before he began his freshman year at Springs University. But, now it was time for the Christmas holidays and Trey was not sure he wanted to go back home. "What do I have to go home to?" he asked himself.

Leaving Home

Trey grew up in a small community in Pennsylvania and was both curious and apprehensive about life at a place like Springs University, a large (26,000 students) university in the South. He had become very close to his parents and younger sister. Even though they were all very busy and ran on different schedules, they made it a point to eat dinner together every night. Trey treasured these times and used them to talk about his daily problems and get their advice on solutions. He knew this family time would be missed the most when he left home for college.

Even more difficult was leaving girl friend, Melissa, behind. She was 16 years old and just beginning her junior year in high school. They had many conversations together about what would happen to them when Trey went off to college. They loved each other and wanted to continue their relationship in spite of the distance that would separate them.

When the time came to leave home, his family drove him to Springs University and helped him move into the residence hall the day it opened. Being there early gave him the chance to adjust to his new surroundings and get to know his roommate. Trey was saddened when the time came for his family to drive back to Pennsylvania.

College Life

That first night was lonely, especially at dinner time. Trey called Melissa and they talked for a while, but she seemed distant. Then she said that she thought it would be best if they were just friends. He was shocked. Only yesterday they had professed undying love for one another, and now it was "just friends!" He wanted to be home so they could talk in person. His loneliness turned to depression.

His roommate moved in the next day and Trey busied himself helping him bring all his stuff up to their room. He knew right away that his new roommate was someone who liked to have fun. And, Trey was ready to experience some college fun.

They partied every night. Really partied. His roommate had a fake ID and Trey asked him to buy a case of beer. During the day Trey sat in his room and drank beer, then at night he went out with his roommate. They quickly made lots of friends.

Fall classes began in the middle of that first week, but Trey continued to party every night with his new friends. On Saturday, a week after he had arrived on campus, Trey opened a textbook for the first time. What he saw was overwhelming. "I can't even read this stuff," he mumbled to himself. In high school Trey had participated in athletics and had not been required to do much school work. It was a small school with winning teams; and teachers allowed special privileges to winning teams. Trey called home to talk to his parents. They talked for nearly three hours while Trey tried to figure out if he really had what it took to be a college student.

The Crash

Midway through the semester, Trey felt that he had gotten himself under control. He began dating another girl and his studies were improving. He made the Spring University baseball reserve team and still had time to pledge a fraternity where he had many new friends. Being away from home was becoming easier.

His parents visited during Parent's Weekend, but it was not a happy reunion. They told him that they were getting a divorce and his father was moving out of the house the very next week. Trey's world began to crash down around him.

A week later, three of Trey's friends from high school were involved in a serious car accident. All three were admitted to the hospital in critical condition. One was on life support and was not expected to survive.

Melissa called with the hope that they could rekindle their relationship. Trey did not tell her that he had begun dating someone else.

The Holidays

As the Christmas holidays approached, Trey thought back on the roller coaster ride his first semester had been. He could not imagine anything being the same back in Pennsylvania. His parents were living in separate houses and not speaking to each other. Three of his friends were in the hospital with serious injuries. Melissa could not decide if she loved him. This would all be so unfamiliar and uncomfortable when he got home. "Where do I go," he asked himself, "when there is no home to go home to?"

Name _____   Date _____

CASE ANALYSIS WORKSHEET

Home Sweet Home

What is this case about? Immerse yourself in this case by imagining that you are Trey Johnson and the news that you have been receiving from back home has not been good. Your parents tell you they are getting divorced, your girlfriend tells your she doesn't want to go with you anymore and three of your high school friends are seriously injured in an auto accident. The Christmas holidays are approaching and you wonder about going home.

Get the facts. List the facts that you know about Trey and his situation:

1. _____

2. _____

3. _____

4. _____

5. _____

State the problem, issue or question that needs to be resolved.

_____

_____

List several ways that the problem might be resolved.

1. _____

2. _____

3. _____

Write down the best way to solve the problem and why you would solve it that way.

_____

_____

CASE STUDY

Another Twist

(This case study was prepared in cooperation with Dawn Wisniewski, Graduate Assistant at the University of South Carolina. It is intended solely to initiate class discussion. All names and some peripheral facts have been disguised.)

As LaTonya Jones hung up the phone with the boyfriend she had left behind at home, she began to cry to herself. The two of them had already endured so much to keep their relationship going, and now she wondered if she had the strength to face yet another twist in life's road.

Friends

LaTonya was a new freshman majoring in nursing at Florence University, an institution with one of the largest minority populations in the southeast. She and William Everly had met in high school and began dating while they were juniors. From the beginning they knew a difficult road lay ahead. LaTonya and William came from different races, but believed they would beat the odds. William had admired her since the beginning of high school, and LaTonya loved the way he made her laugh. To them, love was color blind.

LaTonya and William knew they would face opposition. And, they did. William was called "Tarbaby" and "Niggerlover" at school. LaTonya was accused by her friends of having "sold out" by dating William. It was rough in the beginning, but after everyone became used to the two of them being together, the nature of their relationship seemed to become less important at school.

Family

At home, LaTonya's grandparents were initially hesitant—she had lived with them for several years, and they were very protective of her. But once they got to know William, they welcomed him with open arms. The same was not the case in William's household.

The Everlys had never met LaTonya, but they did not like the idea of their son dating someone outside his race. They worried about what other people would think and say about their family. They wanted William to break up with LaTonya, but William was steadfast that he would not leave her. He was an independent young man who did not need their approval.

The Accident

Something tragic occurred that changed everything. Before high school graduation, William had been on the way over to see LaTonya one Sunday afternoon and was involved in an accident where he totaled his car. Worse, the wreck had paralyzed him from the waist down.

Visits

Now that LaTonya had begun college, it became more difficult to see William, even though she was only an hour away. When she went to visit him, she was only permitted to see him if she brought a friend, and they had to stay outside. The visits were very brief. When William was able to leave the house, one of LaTonya's relatives would pick him up and bring him over to her grandparent's home. The visits became less frequent when William began traveling out of state for rehabilitation treatments.

Perhaps more frustrating was the treatment William received from his mother. She often made comments like, "You're going to rot in that chair" or, "You'll never be able to walk again." She believed that his relationship with LaTonya was the real cause of his accident.

William became jealous and insecure and did not want LaTonya to return to Florence. He pictured her off at college having a great time while he sat at home day after day. He had wanted to go to college himself, but was unable to this year because of his condition. He feared that she would meet someone new and quickly forget him. LaTonya tried to understand why William was so upset. She felt guilty that she was able to lead a normal life while William was confined to his wheel chair. Moreover, she felt somewhat responsible for his accident for not reminding him to wear his seat belt.

As she hung up the phone and wiped the tears that rolled down her checks, LaTonya wondered about her relationship with William. She thought about their hometown, a small town where everyone knows everyone and rumors fly free; about how difficult it had been to keep their relationship, even before the accident; about college and the pressures it brought; about making new college friends; and about friends and family back home. It was all beginning to take its toll on her. She reached for another tissue and murmured to herself, "Can I keep going like this?"

Name _____ Date _____

CASE ANALYSIS WORKSHEET

Another Twist

What is this case about? Imagine yourself in LaTonya Jones' place while she tries to maintain a relationship with her boyfriend from high school.

Get the facts. List the facts that you know about LaTonya and her situation:

1. _____
2. _____
3. _____
4. _____
5. _____

State the problem, issue or question that needs to be resolved.

_____

_____

List several ways that the problem might be resolved.

1. _____
2. _____
3. _____

Write down the best way to solve the problem and why you would solve it that way.

_____

_____

_____

_____

CASE STUDY

Pulling Away

(This case study was prepared in cooperation with Randa Haddad, Residence Director, Furman University, Greenville, South Carolina. It is intended solely to initiate class discussion. All names and some peripheral facts have been disguised.)

Going away to college had not been easy for Richard Lukas. It meant that Tina Miranda would be left behind to finish her senior year of high school. "This is the girl I want to marry," he had told his friends about Tina. It was a commitment that he intended to keep.

Richard had not really wanted to attend Southeastern State University, but it was his father's *alma mater* and his parents had insisted that he continue the tradition. He had gone along not wanting to make a fuss. The University was about a two-hour drive from home and he thought he would spend most of his weekends at home. He really wanted to be at a smaller college closer to home, but this would have to do for the time being.

Richard and Tina had gone together for six months and she was the only woman with whom he had been intimate. His sense of commitment told him that he should not have a sexual relationship with somebody if he could not follow through. With Tina he wanted to follow through. She needed him and he felt responsible for her. He had seen her through some rough emotional times and wanted to take care of her.

Tina had never been good friends with other women. Her friends had always been guys. She communicated by flirting with guys. Richard knew this, but he wanted to overlook it. She made him feel special and that was important to him. He did not want to be just another Joe Schmo, college freshman. He wanted to feel loved.

They had been apart just two weeks when Tina told Richard she thought they should break up. She did not feel she could have friends if she was in a relationship. But, she still wanted them to remain friends.

Richard was hurt. He did not think he could handle just being friends with Tina. He reasoned that it would probably be best if he just started a new life at the university and cut off all ties with Tina. He thought it would probably be best not to allow a past relationship to control his future college life.

Tina saw it differently. She continued to rely on him for emotional and social support even though she did not want to resume their romantic relationship. When he went home, she would show up at his parents' house to talk. He did not even know how she knew he would be home, but she always knew somehow and wanted to talk to him. He felt guilty trying to avoid contact with her because he knew that she had a history of depression and had even attempted suicide twice before she and Richard started dating.

Pulling away from Tina was not so easy. Richard struggled with himself wondering what was the right thing to do.

Name _____ Date _____

CASE ANALYSIS WORKSHEET

Pulling Away

What is this case about? Get into this case by imagining yourself in Richard Lukas' situation of trying to maintain his relationship with Tina Miranda who is a high school senior back home.

Get the facts. List the facts that you know about Richard and Tina's relationship:

1. _____
2. _____
3. _____
4. _____
5. _____

State the problem, issue or question that needs to be resolved.

_____

_____

List several ways that the problem might be resolved.

1. _____
2. _____
3. _____

Write down the best way to solve the problem and why you would solve it that way.

_____

_____

_____

_____

CHAPTER 4

Making New Friends

Overcoming loneliness is a powerful reason for making friends. But, friendship is not merely a way to break from your own solitude. It is, rather, the deepest form of human relationship and the noblest form of human communication, the only one capable of dissolving our loneliness.

Friendships are most likely to form between young people who can make themselves available for friendship and have the youthful energy to pursue deep and meaningful relationships. College is a most opportune time to develop lifelong friendships.

■ Designated Driver

This case depicts the plight of a young freshman in the first week at college when he sees the designated driver for his group of friends drinking beer at the party they were attending. When the party is over and everyone is piling into the jeep for the ride back to campus, he wonders if the driver is really OK to drive and whether it is safe for him to climb in for the ride.

■ The Eating Game

Emily LeBlanc had overcome her own eating disorder so she recognized the symptoms in Jeannie, one of her hall-mates. She wanted to say something to Jeannie, but knew that it would not be an easy thing to do.

■ Late Night

Sally worried about her roommate, Kristina, who went to a party last night and had not yet returned by the time of her 10:00 a.m. class. Sally wondered if she should say something to someone.

■ Should I Leave?

Jennifer Milton is a freshman in journalism at East Coast University. As she reads her entries in the journal she prepared for her freshman seminar class, she realizes how unhappy she is with college and her roommate. She wonders if maybe she should leave.

■ The Lab Partner

Pat Collins had to do all the work in lab. His lab partner just showed up assuming that his work would be done for him. Pat worried about what kind of grade he would get when he had to do everything himself.

■ Treat Me Like a Dummy

A freshman seminar instructor uses an exercise, *Headbands*, to facilitate a discussion on stereotypes. All students in the class have been provisionally admitted to the university and during the discussion, one of them observes that provisionally admitted students are treated like dummies. The instructor sees this to be an unfair label or stereotype when applied to her students and wonders what she should do about it.

■ Just Five More Minutes

A college freshman thinks he might be addicted to the Internet. As a freshman at a large university, he enjoys unlimited access to the Internet for the first time in his life. He takes full advantage of this access, spending more time surfing the 'Net than studying. He and his roommate try to monitor the time each spends on the Internet.

Suggested Readings

Ellis, D. (1997). *Becoming a Master Student*. Boston, MA: Houghton Mifflin Company. Chapter 10.

Ferrett, S. K. (1997). *Peak Performance: Success in College and Beyond*. (2nd Ed). New York: McGraw-Hill. Chapter 12.

Friday, R. A. (1997). "Developing relationships." In Gardner, J. N. & Jewler, A. J. *Your College Experience: Strategies for Success*. Belmont, CA: Wadsworth Publishing Company.

Holkeboen, R. (1996). *Right from the Start: Managing Your College Career*. Belmont, CA: Wadsworth Publishing Company. Chapter 10.

Johnson, N. P., & Johnson, P. E. (1997). "Alcohol, other drugs, and you." In Gardner, J. N., & Jewler, A. J. *Your College Experience: Strategies for Success*. Belmont, CA: Wadsworth Publishing Company.

CASE STUDY

Designated Driver

(This case study was prepared in cooperation with Liz McCormack, Academic Advisor in the College of Nursing at the University of South Carolina. It is intended solely to initiate class discussion. All names and some peripheral facts have been disguised.)

Scott Duncan had just left the fraternity party and stood by the jeep as his friends climbed in. He was sure that none of them were sober enough to drive, but they piled in, laughing and shouting for him to hurry up. He had come with them and now, in a moment's hesitation, he wondered to himself, "Are these guys too drunk?"

First Week as a Freshman

The first week of college at Southern Tech was filled with social opportunities for Scott, a new freshman. He looked like many of his classmates: blonde hair, medium build, average dresser; but was shorter than most at only 5'4". Scott felt like he was entering college with a more mature attitude toward his new independence, compared to the way he saw many of his new friends act. He had made friends with most of the guys on his hall, and they had spent almost every night going out together to parties and clubs. This was a new experience for Scott, and he knew that once classes began, this type of socializing would have to cease. He came to Tech on almost a full scholarship, so he told himself that he would give himself this first week to get all of the partying out of his system so he could focus on his studies for the remainder of the semester.

The party scene was also pretty unfamiliar to Scott. He was not a big drinker in high school. In fact, he was a member of Teen Institute, a teen drug and alcohol prevention program. He had found himself in social drinking situations before, but had usually ended up having to "baby-sit" his friends. He did not consider himself a big party person in high school, and remembered getting drunk only twice; one time, ironically, at a medical leadership conference. Scott did not drink much, but he definitely considered himself a social person and someone who liked to have a good time.

The Fraternity Party

That first weekend, Scott's hallmate, Mike Spenser, invited him and several other guys on his hall to attend an Eta Rho Lambda fraternity party. Some of his hallmates were thinking about rushing this fraternity, so this party gave them the opportunity to meet some of the members and make connections. Scott had not really thought about rushing a fraternity, but this seemed like another good social opportunity before classes began. Scott was very conscious about drunk driving, so he made sure that one of the guys going with them promised to stay sober. Mike volunteered to be the designated driver for the evening. So, Scott and six other guys headed over to the Lambda party, which was being held at the fraternity's off-campus party house. It was about a two-mile drive which took them seven minutes to arrival.

They hopped out of the jeep and headed up the walk to the two-story house. The party was an open house; a chance for everyone to meet each other. Scott was in awe at the amount of beer being served—there must have been 12 kegs lined up against the wall. He felt a little out of place, not really knowing what to do at a fraternity open house. He was underage, but they assured him that he would not be carded to get a beer. He would just have to give a brother his cup and they would fill it up — it was just that simple.

The Designated Driver

Before they left for the party, Scott asked Mike three times if he was sure he wanted to stay sober. Mike assured him that he did. Now, after Scott got his first beer, he noticed that Mike had a cup in his hand. He approached Mike and asked him about his promise to stay sober. Mike promised to have only one beer and remain OK to drive.

At this, Scott thought to himself, "Is he really serious?" Throughout the evening, Scott watched as Mike took one cup and then another and another. Scott himself had three beers and would not even consider driving. Everyone else who came in the jeep was wasted. Scott did not know how many beers Mike had at the party, but he had the feeling that Mike was in no shape to drive. When it was time to head back to campus, Mike reassured Scott and the rest of the guys that he was fine.

As Scott stood ready to climb into the jeep, he could almost hear his own thought, "Should I be doing this?"

Name _____ Date _____

CASE ANALYSIS WORKSHEET

Designated Driver

What is this case about?   Immerse yourself in this case by walking in Scott Duncan's shoes as he decides whether to get into the jeep for the ride back to campus after a fraternity party. He saw the designated driver drinking beer.

Get the facts.   List the facts that you know about Scott and his situation:

1. _____
2. _____
3. _____
4. _____
5. _____

State the problem, issue or question that needs to be resolved.

_____
_____

List several ways that the problem might be resolved.

1. _____
2. _____
3. _____

Write down the best way to solve the problem and why you would solve it that way.

_____
_____
_____
_____

CASE STUDY

The Eating Game

(This case study was prepared in cooperation with Mike Dickinson, Graduate Assistant at the University of South Carolina. It is intended solely to initiate class discussion. All names and some peripheral facts have been disguised.)

Emily had seen all the tricks, and had played most of them herself. She knew the signs of a eating disorder like frequently skipped meals, binge eating, and calorie counting. She had been a master of the eating game, and she suspected her hallmate, Jeannie, was playing it. But, this evening all her doubts were erased when she observed Jeannie's inability to find anything to eat at the dinner table. "Can I let Jeannie continue to play this game?" she whispered to herself.

Overweight

When Emily LeBlanc was 15-years-old and a sophomore in high school, she weighed 160 pounds and realized that she had to go on a diet if she were ever to wear cute outfits and be attractive to boys. Diet she did, and by the time she began her junior year she had lost 20 pounds. She was encouraged by her success and lost another 37 pounds during the first half of her junior year. Still, she saw herself as fat and was intensely afraid of gaining more weight. Her mother thought Emily had lost enough and was so concerned that she took her to a doctor during the winter break. It was then that Emily learned that she might have an eating disorder that caused her to lose weight far beyond what she should have for her height of 5'5". She began seeing a psychologist every week for the next year. During the last half of her senior year, her weight stabilized and she reduced her visits to the doctor to once a month.

The "Freshman Fifteen"

Emily entered South Central State University determined not to gain the "freshman 15," those new pounds that so many freshmen gain during their first few months away from home. She exercised rigorously and ate sparingly to lose 8 pounds after she arrived on campus. She quit seeing her psychologist since that involved driving home. Quite frankly, she enjoyed being away from home and away from her mother's constant questions about her eating. However, when her friends voiced concern about her weight, which had dropped to 108 pounds, she gained "five or maybe three pounds back."

Emily still worried about her weight, but she felt that she handled her eating disorder fairly well. She watched her diet carefully, making sure to get the proper proteins and vitamins. She was pleased that, even though she was not still seeing her doctor, she had not forced herself to throw up since she had been at the University. She had done that at home, but never let her mother know.

The Lunch Bunch

Jeannie lived on the same floor of the residence hall as Emily and shared a room with Sarah, one of Emily's friends. Although Emily and Jeannie were not good friends, they hung out with the same crowd and would often eat meals together with the same group of people. Emily noticed that Jeannie would always complain about being hungry, but would only eat a pretzel or yogurt for lunch. She also noted that Jeannie had started carrying around the special light butter that she herself used for her meals. When Jeannie spoke to her it was usually about exercising or the calories in different foods. Even Sarah expressed concern about Jeannie's eating habits.

Conflict

On this particular evening, Jeannie had just finished another skimpy salad insisting that she could not find anything to eat for dinner. She had eaten the same thing for lunch and Emily knew that there was plenty to eat for dinner including non-fattening foods like broiled chicken breasts and vegetables. In a few minutes the "lunch bunch" would walk back to their residence hall together, as they always did. Emily wondered if she should pull Jeannie aside and say something about her eating behaviors. Pulling her aside would be easy, talking about her eating would be a different story. Jeannie would likely get angry and deny any problems with her eating. As the group rose from their seats, Emily gazed toward the door and struggled with her thoughts. "Should I let her play this game?"

Name _____ Date _____

CASE ANALYSIS WORKSHEET

The Eating Game

What is this case about?   Put yourself in Emily's position and figure out how you would approach Jeannie whom you suspect has an eating disorder.

Get the facts.   List the facts that you know about Emily and the situation she finds herself in:

1. _____
2. _____
3. _____
4. _____
5. _____

State the problem, issue or question that needs to be resolved.

_____

_____

List several ways that the problem might be resolved.

1. _____
2. _____
3. _____

Write down the best way to solve the problem and why you would solve it that way.

_____

_____

_____

_____

CASE STUDY

Late Night

(This case study was prepared in cooperation with Amanda Biggers Leach, Office of Student Affairs, Emory University. It is intended solely to initiate class discussion. All names and some peripheral facts have been disguised.)

Sally sat in her freshman seminar and anxiously awaited the arrival of her roommate, Kristina. It was 10:10 am and Sally had not seen or heard from her since early the night before. As the professor took attendance, Sally's concern escalated. She tried to think of all the possibilities when suddenly her professor asked, "Sally, where's Kristina?"

Sally and Kristina did not know one another when they entered college. They met on the first day of school when they moved into their dorm. However, they were both out-of-state students and found that they had a lot in common. They became friends and got along well as roommates.

Both Sally and Kristina rushed during the first week of school, but Kristina was the only one who pledged. Sally was very busy with cross-country, and did not have a great deal of time to devote to a sorority. While Sally and Kristina maintained their friendship, they also spent time with other students. Kristina, for example, spent time with her new sorority sisters and Sally spent time with other student athletes.

One night Kristina decided to go to a party with some of her new sorority sisters. She told Sally she was leaving, and Sally assumed she would be home later that evening. But when Sally woke up at 7:30 am to get ready for her 9:05 class, she realized Kristina had not been home. This was very odd, especially since Kristina had not mentioned spending the night out. At 8:45 am when Sally left their room to go to class, there was still no sign of Kristina.

Sally's next class at 10:10 was the Freshman seminar. Sally liked this class because it took place in the classroom in her dorm, and Kristina was also enrolled. Before going to class, Sally quickly stopped by her room to see if Kristina had returned, but it did not appear that she had been home. Sally became increasingly concerned, especially since Kristina had never done this before. "I would think she would at least call!" Sally thought to herself. As she walked to her class she hoped Kristina would be there. But, when she got there she did not see Kristina. Her professor knew they were roommates. She wondered if she should say something. Should she voice her concern? Where could she possibly be and why had she not called? These were the thoughts that raced through her mind as she heard the professor ask, "Sally, where is Kristina?"

Name _____   Date _____

CASE ANALYSIS WORKSHEET

Late Night

What is this case about?   Immerse yourself in this case by putting yourself in Kristina's position. She is worried about her roommate who did not come back from a party last night. How would you handle this situation?

Get the facts.   List the facts that you know about Kristina and her situation:

1. _____
2. _____
3. _____
4. _____
5. _____

State the problem, issue or question that needs to be resolved.

_____
_____

List several ways that the problem might be resolved.

1. _____
2. _____
3. _____

Write down the best way to solve the problem and why you would solve it that way.

_____
_____
_____
_____

CASE STUDY

Should I Leave?

(This case study was prepared in cooperation with Leigh Ann Jordan. It is intended solely to initiate class discussion. All names and some peripheral facts have been disguised.)

"This place isn't at all what I expected," thought Jennifer Milton as she read through the entries she had posted to her journal during the past two weeks. Then, talking to herself, she heard the words, "Maybe I should leave."

Classes at East Coast University had been in session for two weeks and Jenny, a freshman, was not completely adjusted to her new life as a university student. She had done very well in high school and decided to go away for college. The decision had been difficult because she was close to her parents and her shyness left her apprehensive about living with a roommate whom she had never known and making a whole new set of friends. But, East Coast's journalism school was one of the best and she realized that she would have to leave home and her home state of Maryland to take advantage of it.

She re-read the first entry she had written for the journal she was required to keep in her Freshman Seminar class:

> *August 25*—*Well, I've officially been here for one week and am amazed that I am still alive. I honestly have to say that this has been the hardest week of my life. Besides being extremely introverted, I have a roommate who is the complete opposite of myself. I have noticed that the other people in my hall have latched onto their roommates or already know people here but my roommate has been gone every night partying and I have had difficulty prying myself from the room. I have met a few nice people on my floor and other places but not one quite like my old friends or people I normally hang out with. I am yet to meet one person who does not drink and party, except for myself. The only way I think I have continued on is by having constant contact with my friends and family back home. I know these first few weeks are expected to be hell but I keep asking myself, "Why?" I mean I am essentially here to go to journalism school, but I can do that anywhere.*

Jenny reflected back to that first few days and again the pain of feeling left out and being far away from her parents rose up within her. She wondered if that feeling would ever go away. She read her next entry:

> *August 26*—*Well, the atmosphere has definitely changed here. The pace has quickened in my classes but I feel that I am right up to speed with it. No excessive stress, yet. I wonder how other people are able to handle it because they seem to be going out all the time or partying and I barely have enough time to complete the work and make sure I'm on top of things. Yesterday, I swam laps at the P.E. center and it was such a relief. Whenever I have some spare time I will have to go back and do that because it cleared my head so much.*

Today my English teacher changed. Apparently the old one just got up on Friday, jumped on a bus and went home. Boy, I wish I could do that! But I really, really like this new professor. His ideas make sense to me. He told us today to not accept everything that people hand us. Instead examine it and question it, put it through our own "filters." I really think I am going to learn a lot from this professor.

"I'm still learning a lot from him," she thought. The thought warmed her.

"People like him are what college was supposed to be about. Why can't I just let that be my answer," she wondered as she turned to the entry she had made during the second week of class:

September 3—OK, I know these first two weeks are supposed to be hard; homesickness, feeling left out, etc. . . . but I really feel like it's time for a change. I've already discussed with my family the option of transferring next semester. The two schools I'm interested in have excellent journalism programs, actually one is ranked in the top 10 in the country. I applied to the other but decided against it because it was only a half-an-hour away from my home—I really thought I was brave enough to leave my entire life behind. Now I realize how much I really liked who I was and how much I hate how this school makes me feel. But, so far, with all this free time, I have just centered my every spare moment on school and I am hoping that my grades will be sufficient. I never applied to that one school because I was afraid my grades weren't high enough.

"Should I leave?" Jenny got caught up in the thought. She knew her parents would never say anything about her coming back home so soon after leaving for college, but her friends might wonder.

"Would they think I failed?" she mused. The thought struck her that they might all wish they could do the same thing. She smiled to herself as she pictured all of her friends running into each other at the mall and lying about why they had only lasted two weeks in college. She continued reading:

September 4—I know that my roommate and I are from completely opposite ends of the spectrum and I haven't even hinted that we hang out or be friends once but I thought that at least I could live with her. After today I have found this to be extremely difficult. In the beginning I was upset because she partied all the time and would come home in the middle of the night and wake me up because she was drunk and clumsy. Then I had to listen to her stories in the morning of how "wasted" she was and act like I cared. Well, it eventually got to the point that she didn't like me waking her up in the morning when I had class, so lately she's been staying over with other people. Well, for the past, I guess, about two weeks, I have on and off been receiving prank calls in the middle of the night. Last Saturday at 3:30 am I received a really upsetting one and I have no idea how this guy knows my name because I have not met <u>any</u> guys yet. One day he left me a message on my answering machine so I guess he got my name from that. So I decided to change the memo to a song playing. My roommate got very upset and I told her why I didn't want my name on there so then she changed it to: "Hi, you've reached Susan's room, otherwise known as Lush, leave a message." Well, a friend of mine from Texas called and didn't know if she had dialed the right number so I changed the message to "Hi, you've reached 555-3456, we're not in right now so please leave a message." She got really p—— o——, left the room and we've been avoiding each other since. Oh well.

Name _____   Date _____

CASE ANALYSIS WORKSHEET

Should I Leave?

What is this case about?   Put yourself in Jennifer Milton's place as you read the entries she has written in her journal. She is unhappy with her roommate and thinks about leaving college.

Get the facts.   List the facts that you know about Jennifer and her situation:

1. _____
2. _____
3. _____
4. _____
5. _____

State the problem, issue or question that needs to be resolved.

_____

_____

List several ways that the problem might be resolved.

1. _____
2. _____
3. _____

Write down the best way to solve the problem and why you would solve it that way.

_____

_____

_____

_____

CASE STUDY

The Lab Partner

(This case study was prepared in cooperation with Lori Bumgarner, Assistant Director of Academic Services, Methodist College, and Corbin Smythe, Director of Co-curricular Activities, University of Indianapolis. It is intended solely to initiate class discussion. All names and some peripheral facts have been disguised.)

Pat Collins reluctantly handed in his lab assignment to the teaching assistant. The lab today had been a complete disaster, and Pat worried that his grade would begin to be affected by the poor work that he and his lab partner were performing. But Pat had to do all of the work himself while his partner just showed up to class assuming that everything would be done for him. "I can't go on like this," Pat thought, "I'll never get a good grade if I am forced to do everything myself."

Pat was in the middle of his first semester at Mercury University. He came to MU from Maryland with a very good academic record, and decided to major in pharmacy after his experience working part-time in a drug store while in high school. He knew college would be challenging but did not know exactly how challenging it would be. Regardless, Pat was coming to school to study—not to party—so he was ready to accept the challenge.

During the first couple of weeks of the semester, Pat was without a lab partner for his chemistry class. A very conscientious student, he was worried that not having a lab partner would require additional work and would affect his grade. He had already called his mother to tell her that he had done poorly on a biology test, so he felt that he could not afford more work than would have been the case if he had a lab partner. But, Pat was very particular, so not having a partner allowed him to do the lab work exactly like he wanted it done. Two weeks into the course, Pat was finally assigned a partner and figured that things would begin to fall into place. But, instead of falling into place, things began to fall apart.

Pat's new lab partner was never prepared for class. He never read over the experiments or material before class and did not attend recitations. He did not study nor take any of the quizzes. He just came to the lab each week without any idea of how to perform the experiments. Unlike Pat, he was not in the least concerned about getting good grades. Pat wondered, "How can I possibly survive this semester in lab with this slacker?"

This week's experiment did not work the way it was supposed to and Pat blamed his lab partner's lack of preparation. Pat tried to save the experiment (without his partner's help), but it still did not come out right. That was not all; chemical problems and equations also had to be completed before the end of lab. Pat knew how to do the problems, but the failed experiment made doing the equations correctly much more difficult. As he worked through the problems he could feel the clock ticking away the time; he was running out of time.

Pat felt frustrated and angry. He was already in a bad mood when he arrived in lab, feeling tired and a little homesick. He missed his friends and family in Maryland. Making friends at Mercury was not as easy as he would like because he saw himself as somewhat more quiet and conservative than most others at the university. He did not really want to alienate his lab partner, and did his best not to be rude even though he was angry. He kept from confronting him because he was afraid that would make it too awkward to work with him in the future.

Pat turned in the assignment expecting a bad grade. The teaching assistant noticed the frustration and asked what was going on. Pat hesitated as he struggled for a way to respond.

Name _____ Date _____

CASE ANALYSIS WORKSHEET

The Lab Partner

What is this case about? Get into the case by putting yourself in Pat Collins' place as he tries to figure out what to do about his lab partner who won't do any of the work.

Get the facts. List the facts that you know about Pat and his situation:

1. _____
2. _____
3. _____
4. _____
5. _____

State the problem, issue or question that needs to be resolved.

_____

_____

List several ways that the problem might be resolved.

1. _____
2. _____
3. _____

Write down the best way to solve the problem and why you would solve it that way.

_____

_____

_____

_____

CASE STUDY

Treat Me Like a Dummy

(This case study was prepared in cooperation with Penny Woodcock, Southern Methodist University. It is intended solely to initiate class discussion. All names and some peripheral facts have been disguised.)

Patricia Rider was taken aback by what she was hearing. It had never occurred to her that the freshmen in her University 101 class were treated like dummies. They seemed so bright and energetic; so excited to learn. Yet, they were telling her that, at this university, they received little respect from faculty or students. It was not fair and she wanted to do something about it.

Patty, as she liked to call herself, was a residence hall director who taught a freshman seminar course at a large university in the South. Her eight o'clock class students were sometimes painfully difficult to wake up. But, today it had been different. The discussion was vigorous and Patty was excited by the thoughtfulness of her students' comments.

Most of the comments came during the processing of an exercise called "Headbands." The objective of the activity was to stimulate thinking and discussion about diversity and stereotypes in society, specifically on college campuses. The participants were given an exercise to complete on their own. In this case it was a NASA exercise that required the students to rank in importance the items that would be needed on an expedition to the lighted side of the moon. Once individuals ranked the items on their own, they were given a headband to wear that stated how others were to treat them.

The students were instructed not to tell each other what the headband said, but to react from that point on according to what was written on the headband. Ten headbands were used with the following statements:

- Treat me like I'm important

- Treat me like a dummy

- Disagree with me

- Agree with me

- Laugh at me

- Obey me

- Ignore me

- Ask my advice

- Pity me

- Support me

- (Blank, with nothing written)

Once given their headbands, the students were instructed to complete the same activity as a group, reaching a group consensus while still reacting to the headband statements. The remaining students were asked to watch the group members and chart their reactions throughout the activity.

During the activity the group reacted as one would expect. The student with the "Ignore me" headband withdrew from the discussion after his suggestion was completely overlooked, "Agree with me" became more and more involved in the discussion with each affirmation, and "Treat me like I'm important" took over the show in her new-found leader role.

Once the group had reached a consensus, Patty went around the circle and asked each participant their reaction to the exercise.

"Did you feel like a part of the group?" she asked. "How did other's reactions to you impact your involvement in the activity?" "Can you guess what your headband said?"

In an attempt to relate to the students' own lives, Patty asked for the students to name various groups that "wear" the labels that appeared on the headbands. The students said that they put the blank headband on people with disabilities and the homeless. Because people are unsure of how to react to these individuals, they are simply overlooked. The class agreed that upper-class students are a group from whom they asked advice, citing that they had experience in college life and therefore their thoughts and ideas could be trusted.

One by one the students shared their insights and reactions to the activity. It was not until the headband "Treat me like a dummy" was discussed that Patty was surprised by an observation. When that student was asked what groups on campus are treated like dummies, she quickly replied, "The Provisional Year (PY) students."

That comment resulted in a rush of affirming remarks from the other students. All of these students felt like they were labeled "dummy" by their peers, professors, and the campus community as a whole.

One student asked the question, "Why else would all the PY classes be held down by the gymnasium on the edge of campus?" It seemed obvious to the students that the group that mattered was the respected Honors College, tucked away in the center of campus and given the best facilities.

This was the first time Patty had heard these sentiments in class. Soon after the first class meeting, Patty had forgotten that these students were in the Provisional Year program. Expecting to have a group of first-generation college students, Patty was surprised that their writing and communication skills were, for the most part, excellent and that their comments were bright and thoughtful. Soon the Provisional Year title lost any importance. As a matter of fact, it was not until a class visit from an advisor, that she truly understood the purpose and background of the Provisional Year program.

According to the advisor, this same group of students in previous years would have been admitted to the university without stipulation. However, last year the university made a push to raise admissions standards. As a result of the new standards, these students were no longer given a chance at automatic acceptance. The fact that they were in the PY program was most likely due to a low score on one of the three elements of the admissions formula: GPA, class rank, or SAT score. A low standing on one of these could have made the difference between regular or provisional year acceptance. For example, a student who had an excellent class rank and a high GPA but did not do well on standardized tests, would be accepted into the PY program. One more example may be a student who came from an extremely competitive high school who just did not rank high enough to be considered. These students did not need remedial help and were not generally first-generation college students.

Once in the PY program, students registered from a list of PY courses that have small enrollment and are taught by hand-selected professors. Successful completion of two semesters with at least a C average resulted in the Provisional Year stipulation being dropped from the student's transcript.

Despite the initial stereotypes and assumptions Patty had of the class, she taught it as she would have any other University 101 class. What she heard seemed so unfair. She wondered what she could do.

Name _____   Date _____

CASE ANALYSIS WORKSHEET

Treat Me Like a Dummy

What is this case about? Immerse yourself in this case by imagining that you are one of the students that feel they are being treated like dummies at the university. What do you think your instructor should do about the situation?

Get the facts. List the facts that you know about this case:

1. _____

2. _____

3. _____

4. _____

5. _____

State the problem, issue or question that needs to be resolved.

_____

_____

List several ways that the problem might be resolved.

1. _____

2. _____

3. _____

Write down the best way to solve the problem and why you would solve it that way.

_____

_____

_____

_____

CASE STUDY

Just Five More Minutes

(This case study was prepared in cooperation with Sandra Hughes, Administrative Assistant in the College of Journalism and Mass Communications, and Kimberly Dennis, a Graduate Assistant at the University of South Carolina. It is intended solely to initiate class discussion. All names and some peripheral facts have been disguised.)

"Time's up!" Matt's roommate announced.

"OK, OK. Just five more minutes," Matt replied.

Matt's conscience gnawed at him. "I've got to get off the Internet and start my homework," he thought, but something kept him glued to his seat, staring at the incandescent glow of the screen. He was absolutely mesmerized. As a freshman at a large university in the South, this was really the first time that Matt had unlimited access to the Internet. In high school, the only time he had access to a computer was at school, and then it was on a very limited basis. Now, after being exposed to e-mail and the Internet through his University 101 class, he was a frequent surfer of the 'Net.

During the first few weeks of school, Matt found himself going to the computer lab in the library to check his e-mail and would wind up spending up to two hours surfing the Internet, mostly exploring professional wrestling sites. "This is way too inconvenient," he told his father. "I have to spend too much time going back and forth from the library. It would make a lot more sense if you could just get a computer for me to have in my dorm room."

Shortly thereafter, Matt's dad purchased a computer for his residence hall room. While this definitely saved Matt the time it took him to travel back and forth to the library, it also provided him with twenty-four hour access to feed what was quickly becoming a compulsion to be on the Internet. He and his roommate tried to monitor the time that each other spent on the Internet, but Matt still spent more time on the computer than he spent studying. He often spent a lot of time on the 'Net in the afternoon, then got off to study for a while, and then got back on in the evening.

When Matt went away to college, his parents were concerned about his study habits. He never really had to study very hard to make good grades in school, and his parents were worried that he would be in for a rude awakening in college. He reassured them every weekend when he went home however, that "... the lowest grade I've made has been B minuses on one test and one assignment. That's pretty good for college!"

Matt's parents were also concerned that he would have trouble meeting people and making friends. His girlfriend of two years, Donna, attended the Governor's School, an elite private school. "We know how much Donna means to you and how close you two are," his parents said. "We just don't want you to spend all your time missing her and not making any new friends at college."

"I do miss Donna a lot," Matt thought to himself, as he recalled his parent's words. But it was good that they could keep in touch via e-mail. "I'm not using the Internet as a replacement for going out with friends, though," Matt thought to himself out loud.

"Five minutes is up!" his roommate called out again, interrupting his thoughts.

"It's just a fun and interesting thing to do . . ." Matt continued to rationalize his time spent on the Internet as he tried to block out the thought that he might have an addiction.

Name _____ Date _____

CASE ANALYSIS WORKSHEET

Just Five More Minutes

What is this case about? Immerse yourself in this case by taking on the identity of Matt who thinks he might be addicted to the Internet.

Get the facts. List the facts that you know about Matt and his situation:

1. _____
2. _____
3. _____
4. _____
5. _____

State the problem, issue or question that needs to be resolved.

_____
_____

List several ways that the problem might be resolved.

1. _____
2. _____
3. _____

Write down the best way to solve the problem and why you would solve it that way.

_____
_____
_____
_____

CHAPTER 5

Professors and Staff

The men and women who have dedicated themselves to teaching in colleges and universities love the subjects they teach. They have studied for years and have gained deep knowledge of their subject, which they strongly desire to share with students. As one student observed, "Professors are not all trying to ruin our lives—they're on our side."

Relationships between students and faculty are usually most productive and satisfying when based on honesty, promise-keeping, respect for persons and fairness.

■ Wounded Freshman

In this case, Ann Williamson is angry and embarrassed when her English instructor criticizes her paper in front of the class.

■ The Speech Instructor

This is a case about a freshman who felt falsely accused by her instructor for talking in class. Humiliated and angry, she spoke back and now is trying to find a way to apologize.

■ On the Fringe

A new freshman's appearance led his instructor to believe that he was a drug user. At the end of one class session, the instructor told the student that she did not appreciate him coming to her class stoned. The student was shocked and tried to find something to say.

■ Speak English

Roger Huffman was an engineering major who took a music appreciation course from an instructor who had a heavy accent. Roger did not feel he was getting much out of the class because he could not understand the instructor. In his freshman orientation class, he asked the question, "Would it be rude to just ask a professor to speak English?"

■ The Flooded Room

Caroline Willis returned to her dorm room to find it flooded for the third time. "What do I do now," she thought.

■ Bureaucracy

A freshman, who is not completely familiar with the university library, tries on his own to find materials he needs for a paper. When he is unsuccessful, he asks a librarian who says she is busy and sends him away. He finds another librarian who is on the phone. When she finishes her conversation, he starts to ask her, but she interrupts to say, "Can't you see I'm on my break?" Humiliated and angry, he leaves the building wondering what went wrong.

Suggested Readings

Ferrett, S. K. (1997). *Peak Performance: Success in College and Beyond.* New York: McGraw-Hill. Chapter 3.

Jewler, A. J., & Gardner, J. N. (1997). "Professor and student: Partners in learning." In Gardner, J. N., & Jewler, A. J. *Your College Experience: Strategies for Success.* Belmont, CA: Wadsworth Publishing Company. 127-137.

Sherfield, R. M., Williamson, J. C., & McCandrew, D. A. (1997). *Roadways to Success.* Needham, MA: Allyn and Bacon. Chapter 10.

CASE STUDY

Wounded Freshman

(This case study was prepared in cooperation with Jill Garon, Victor McCormick Hall Director, Marquette University. It is intended solely to initiate class discussion. All names and some peripheral facts have been disguised.)

Ann Williamson wanted to run out of class and go as far away as her legs would carry her. She had just been "called out" by her English instructor in front of the whole class and was boiling with anger and embarrassment. "Is this the way they treat freshmen?" she wondered as she tried to control the hurt she felt.

Ann was one of 20 freshmen in English 101, English Composition. It was a special class for the limited number of students who had been admitted to the university on probation. Each of these students were required to complete a prescribed curriculum of 30 semester hours with a C grade average during their freshman year in order to continue their studies at the university. It was a "all or nothing" chance to prove themselves. Ann felt the pressure. She had never enjoyed school and always found it difficult. High academic achievement was not one of her strengths and she knew that she would have to work hard and focus a lot of attention on her grades.

It was the end of September, about a month past the last day to add or drop classes, Dr. Elizabeth Olsen, her English professor and academic adviser, had assigned the class to write a personal reflection paper about a lesson they had learned at some point in their lives. Ann was unsure about what to write. As usual, she felt that Dr. Olsen's instructions were unclear. She always seemed to make vague assignments and was unwilling to elaborate when asked for clarification. The students had quit asking. Instead, they just guessed at what they thought she might want. They had learned that she would somehow make them look stupid if they asked. In a condescending tone she would say, "Sweetheart" (she never used a student's name), "you'll never get out of here if you can't understand simple instructions. No one's going to hold your hand. You just have to figure some things out on your own."

Everyone in class tried to "lay low" and keep from being noticed. But, Dr. Olsen required that students bring their first draft to class and she would quickly read and comment on it. That could be a mortifying experience. Ann heard her tell a classmate, "Honey, this is not what I'm looking for. You need to start over from scratch."

Ann felt herself begin to panic. She was not comfortable with the paper she had written and did not want Dr. Olsen to read it just yet. Dr. Olsen must have seen her expression and began moving in her direction. Ann, usually very quiet in class, blurted out, "I'm not sure this is what you wanted."

Dr. Olsen picked up Ann's paper and began scanning it. "The caliber of this work is pretty low. Actually, it's just trash," she commented loudly.

Upset and embarrassed, Ann looked down at her desk with a desperate thought, "Please no, not in front of the class."

Name _____ Date _____

CASE ANALYSIS WORKSHEET

Wounded Freshman

What is this case about? Immerse yourself in this case by putting yourself in Ann Williamson's place. She has just been criticized by her instructor in front of the class.

Get the facts. List the facts that you know about Ann and her situation:

1. _____
2. _____
3. _____
4. _____
5. _____

State the problem, issue or question that needs to be resolved.

_____

_____

List several ways that the problem might be resolved.

1. _____
2. _____
3. _____

Write down the best way to solve the problem and why you would solve it that way.

_____

_____

_____

_____

PROFESSORS AND STAFF

CASE STUDY

The Speech Instructor

(This case study was prepared in cooperation with Robin Inglehart, Residence Director at Marquette University, and Kim Dennis, University of Utah. It is intended solely to initiate class discussion. All names and some peripheral facts have been disguised.)

"You should shut up and quit talking and pay attention!" the Speech instructor yelled at Brenda.

Brenda's blood boiled. Pointing to her notebook, she yelled back, "Look, I wrote down what you just said. It's not fair for you to accuse me like that! This is bulls——!"

On the way to her next class Brenda's blood continued to boil. "How dare he accuse me like that, in front of the whole class, when I wasn't even the one talking this time," she muttered out loud.

When she got to her next class, University 101, she asked the graduate assistant through tightened lips, "Did you ever get into trouble in class when you were in college?" Sensing that something was wrong, the graduate assistant asked what had happened. Brenda began to explain, emphasizing that she "really wasn't the one talking this time."

This was Brenda's first year at a large university. She considered herself intelligent, but did not do as well on her SATs as she knew she could. So, she was admitted to the university on a provisional basis. Despite her provisional status, Brenda was determined to make good grades. She always participated in class and was not afraid to speak out on her opinions and ideas. Her social nature led her to talk easily to others in class and she usually managed to find several classmates who supported her ideas. Most found her entertaining.

As she sat in her usual front row seat in University 101, her mind swam with scattered thoughts about the day's beginning, and what she still had left to do before the day's end. "This morning stunk! I'm in a bad mood now for the rest of the day," she thought. "As if today hasn't started off bad enough, I still have to pick up my two younger brothers and then go the work at Chick-Fil-A tonight."

Brenda lived at home with her mother, father and two younger brothers, one of whom was in the first grade and the other in third. She often helped her mother out by picking them up from school and watching them until her mother got home from work.

As she continued to sift through her thoughts, she still could not believe how her speech instructor had treated her. "I have never been so humiliated in my entire life. And to do it in front of the entire class . . . how could he?"

Then she began to wonder how her grade might be affected; she had to get good grades if she wanted to remain at the university and have her provisional status removed.

"Maybe it wasn't such a good idea for me to yell back at him," she thought. "I guess I could apologize to him, but he owes me an apology, too! I wonder how I can do this whole apology thing?"

Name _____ Date _____

CASE ANALYSIS WORKSHEET

The Speech Instructor

What is this case about? Place yourself in Brenda's position when she finds herself yelling back at her instructor when she feels falsely accused of talking in class.

Get the facts. List the facts that you know about Brenda and her situation:

1. _____
2. _____
3. _____
4. _____
5. _____

State the problem, issue or question that needs to be resolved.

_____

_____

List several ways that the problem might be resolved.

1. _____
2. _____
3. _____

Write down the best way to solve the problem and why you would solve it that way.

_____

_____

_____

_____

CASE STUDY

On the Fringe

(This case study was prepared in cooperation with Virginia Welsh, University of California at Santa Cruz. It is intended solely to initiate class discussion. All names and some peripheral facts have been disguised.)

Randal Corrigan still had not gotten himself together. He had overslept and been late for class, but he did not think he looked that bad! As class ended and he arose to leave, the professor looked at him and said, "I don't appreciate having you come to my class stoned."

Randal knew he was disorganized. Even his curly hair was out of control. His clothes were rumpled too; he was in a hurry this morning and had quickly grabbed his shirt off the floor and put on the same jeans he had worn yesterday. A fast bike ride to campus, his book bag slung over his shoulder, had not gotten him to his 12:00 noon class on time.

He was only a few minutes late and the class was off to a slow start anyway. They were doing lifelines and discussion on whatever subject students wanted to talk about. It was not a tightly structured class. It just rolled along, with its direction determined mostly by the students themselves. And, that was appropriate for a class like this; one that tried to introduce freshmen to the university with all of its many learning resources and opportunities, and to each other and an instructor who could help them adjust to their new learning environment.

Ms. Florence Daniels (she liked to be called "Flo") worked in the campus bookstore and had been teaching University 101 for several years. She had a degree in social work and worked in a college of nursing at one time. Her classes were always described as very casual. Students felt free to say what they were thinking and felt safe asking questions; it was a trusting place. Students trusted one another enough to let their guard down and share personal things about their lives. It certainly was not like other classes taught at the university.

Randal liked the class. He was very active, always participating and having fun. He was never without some little comment, but never rude or disrespectful. He looked a little "on the fringe" in his crumpled clothes with funky jewelry and uncontrollable hair. "I guess I must look like a stoner," Randal told his friends, "Everybody just assumes I smoke pot."

His only experience with marijuana was in high school. He tried it once and did not like it because it made him sick. He never tried it again. But, teachers and acquaintances had accused him of doing drugs on more than one occasion. He never quite understood why, except that the way he looked must just say to people, "Hey, look, this guy is a pot head."

And now "Flo" was on his case.

Class had just ended. Other students were milling about as they made their way to the door. Ms. Daniels walked over to Randal's desk and said, "I don't appreciate you coming to my class stoned. It is illegal and harmful." Heads turned to see to whom she was speaking.

Shocked, Randal searched for something to say.

Name _____   Date _____

CASE ANALYSIS WORKSHEET

On the Fringe

What is this case about?   This case asks that you see yourself as a freshman whose appearance led his instructor to believe he was a drug user. How could you convince the instructor otherwise?

Get the facts.   List the facts that you know about Randal and his situation:

1. _____

2. _____

3. _____

4. _____

5. _____

State the problem, issue or question that needs to be resolved.

_____

_____

List several ways that the problem might be resolved.

1. _____

2. _____

3. _____

Write down the best way to solve the problem and why you would solve it that way.

_____

_____

_____

_____

CASE STUDY

Speak English

(This case study was prepared in cooperation with Kyle Pendleton, Coordinator of Greek Affairs, Columbia University. It is intended solely to initiate class discussion. All names and some peripheral facts have been disguised.)

Roger Huffman's University 101 instructor seemed to be someone who would understand. At least he spoke English. He was just now starting the second class session of the semester and he was doing it by getting the class to talk about their first week's experiences in the university. Roger heard the question, "How's everything going so far?" and wondered if it would be right for him to speak up.

Roger had always been one to speak his mind. But, now he was in college and he was not sure that it was OK to say the first thing that popped into his head. He did that in high school and once made his senior English teacher so angry that she threw a book at him. He did not want that to happen in college. Besides, people here seemed a lot smarter and appeared to be much more thoughtful about what they said in class. "Think before you speak," he said to himself. That was going to be his new policy.

Roger had spent his whole life in small to medium-sized towns in South Carolina. His parents divorced when he was four and he moved with his mother from Clover, with its 3,500 residents, to Aiken where about 14,000 people lived. Neither town had as many people as the university with its 26,000 students. His mother remarried and he grew up with an older step-brother and a younger half-brother. He was the only one of his brothers with red hair and his smaller size always found him the last chosen in neighborhood pick-up games. But, he loved the outdoors and was the best hunter in the family. He liked to water ski and had become better at it than any of his friends.

The activity where he excelled more than any other was band. He played trumpet in his middle school band and later continued to play for his high school marching band. His band experience had afforded him his only opportunity to travel outside of South Carolina. He had been to Key West and to Texas with the band, but the most exciting trip had been to London where the band competed with some of the British Isle's best marching bands.

Roger had decided to come to the university because of the fine reputation of its marching band. He did not get a band scholarship, but he really never wanted to attend any other university.

He had decided to major in engineering because he enjoyed math and he knew that there were good, high-paying jobs for those who completed degrees in this field. He had enrolled in five courses including English composition, pre-calculus math, chemistry, music appreciation and, of course, University 101. The English course caused him the most anxiety. He had never forgotten the high school teacher who had thrown the book at him and still felt uncomfortable in an English class. As a matter of fact, when he had gone to the bookstore to buy his English textbook, he had a nose bleed that he attributed to the anxiety he still felt whenever he thought about English.

At the university, English had not turned out to be his worst course. Music appreciation was the nightmare. The professor in this class was a foreigner with an accent so heavy he could not be understood by any of the freshmen in the class. The professor's name was Dr. Kostrzewa and he was from one of those countries in Central Europe that used to be part of the Soviet Union. He was probably a brilliant musician, but Roger did not feel that it did him much good because he could not understand a word the man said as he filled the chalk board with one piece of music after another.

He had never had any difficulty dealing with people who were different than him and whose lives had been lived in parts of the world of which he had no knowledge. In high school he had met exchange students from all over the world and was comfortable with "open-minded liberals, racist rednecks, good sports teams, and talented artists" as he had once described the diversity he experienced there. Difference was not his problem, language was.

"I can't understand a single word he says," he thought to himself. "I wonder if anyone else in this class has a problem like that? Now is my chance, should I bring it up? Would it be rude to just ask a professor to speak English?"

Name _____   Date _____

CASE ANALYSIS WORKSHEET

Speak English

What is this case about?   Many students will find it easy to identify with Roger Huffman as he tries to deal with a professor who has a heavy foreign accent.

Get the facts.   List the facts that you know about Roger and his predicament:

1. _____
2. _____
3. _____
4. _____
5. _____

State the problem, issue or question that needs to be resolved.

_____
_____

List several ways that the problem might be resolved.

1. _____
2. _____
3. _____

Write down the best way to solve the problem and why you would solve it that way.

_____
_____
_____
_____

CASE STUDY

The Flooded Room

(This case study was prepared in cooperation with Andrea Wyrosdick, Director of Residential Life, Converse College. It is intended solely to initiate class discussion. All names and some peripheral facts have been disguised.)

Caroline Willis returned from her quick midnight adventure to the beach and saw the orange-brown water oozing under her door and spreading across the floor of her dorm room. "This is the third flood in a month. This can't be happening again," she thought.

Taylor Hall

Caroline had just begun her freshman classes at Dunhill College and felt lucky to be in the first group of students to move back into the freshly restored and remodeled Taylor Hall. Taylor was one of the old buildings on campus. It was originally built during an extensive building program on campus launched in the late 1930s as part of the New Deal. Named for the Reverend Jonathon Taylor (1768-1820), first president of Dunhill College, the building had become rundown and neglected in the last decade or so. Recently, it was closed for a complete overhaul. During the year and a half it took to renovate, the building was first gutted, leaving only the roof, floors and exterior walls. Then it was transformed from within into a new and modern residence hall.

Caroline was comfortable in the "new" Taylor Hall. The residents were focused academically and took full advantage of the ample learning opportunities in existence at Dunhill College. Caroline, though undecided about her major, enrolled in the Liberal Arts and defined herself as a student eager to learn whatever she could. She was conscientious about her grades and made academic success her highest priority. She fit well into the culture of Taylor Hall.

Choosing to attend Dunhill College came easily as she was awarded a State scholarship. Prior to this decision, Caroline hoped to leave the small town she was raised in and go far away. Instead, she chose Dunhill College which was two hours from home.

The Floods

Early in September, Caroline sat paralyzed as she watched water stream down her walls. The sprinklers on the third floor had malfunctioned. Water damaged Caroline's personal belongings including text books. The most severe damage was to her computer tower. The College offered to have the Division of Computer Services inspect the tower. Not only did Dunhill College inspect and replace belongings, but also they immediately cleaned and dried the walls.

CHAPTER FIVE

In late September, Caroline was up late studying for her calculus quiz when she decided to get a snack from the canteen. Her corner room in the basement was a few feet from the canteen so she didn't have far to walk. As she opened the door to the canteen, she saw the orange-brown water rushing in through the outside door. She quickly warned her hallmates, returned to her room and lifted her belongings to safety. "Thank goodness I had time to save my stuff," she thought. College workers cleaned the rooms and built wooden pallets for residents to place their belongings on.

A few days later on a Saturday evening, Caroline and some friends spontaneously went to the beach for a few hours. They went to escape the stress of the week and the unusually long period of rain that had enveloped the Dunhill College area. They were frustrated and had grown impatient about the state of this newly renovated residence hall. At the beach they could relax, if even for a few hours.

When they returned at 6 am, Caroline was welcomed by the muddy water spreading across her room. Sinking into her bed, she looked around the room to see her computer tower sitting in water. "Now what?" she murmured.

Name _____ Date _____

CASE ANALYSIS WORKSHEET

The Flooded Room

What is this case about? If you were Caroline Willis and your dorm room was flooded for the third time in this newly renovated residence hall, how would you handle the situation?

Get the facts. List the facts that you know about Caroline and the situation she finds herself in:

1. _____
2. _____
3. _____
4. _____
5. _____

State the problem, issue or question that needs to be resolved.

_____
_____

List several ways that the problem might be resolved.

1. _____
2. _____
3. _____

Write down the best way to solve the problem and why you would solve it that way.

_____
_____
_____
_____

PROFESSORS AND STAFF

CASE STUDY

Bureaucracy

(This case study was prepared in cooperation with Catherine Bell, Graduate Assistant at the University of South Carolina. It is intended solely to initiate class discussion. All names and some peripheral facts have been disguised.)

Jamie Huston certainly did not expect the librarian to respond that way. He was polite and courteous like he had been brought up; she was just plain rude.

It was an OK day, but again Jamie, an 18-year-old freshman, had waited until the last minute to begin his assignment. He had a two-page paper due first thing tomorrow morning and he had not even begun. "Why do I always find myself in these situations?" he wondered as he walked toward the university's library.

Jamie was a good student with a habit of procrastinating. As he approached the library he thought about how much he hated going there. The library was huge and he was never sure where they kept the stuff he needed. "I hate this place," he thought as he climbed the steps, "Everyone looks at me like I'm some kind of helpless freshman idiot."

He entered and walked around looking for the newspaper room. He saw no signs pointing the way, but he did see someone at the desk under the "Reference" sign. He thought to himself, "Ask, Stupid."

Approaching the desk, he asked politely, "Excuse me, can you tell me where the newspaper room is?"

The woman looked up and replied abruptly, "I'm busy. Go ask someone else."

Shocked at such a short and curt response, Jamie walked away determined to find the room himself.

From the library tour during freshman orientation, Jamie vaguely remembered that the newspaper room was up several floors. He found the elevator and punched the button to the fifth floor; he would begin looking there. As he rode he wondered, "What was her problem? Maybe she'd had a bad day. But, that's no excuse. She didn't have to take it out on me. I'm just a helpless, red-headed, freckle-faced freshman who's scared of a big bad library." He was smiling to himself when the elevator door opened.

The newspaper room was not on the fifth floor, so Jamie walked down to the fourth. And there he found it. He was supposed to find out what was going on in the world the day he was born and write a short summary. "I suppose any newspaper will do," he thought, "all I need to do is find one from the right date."

He spotted a librarian at her desk. She was on the phone, so he decided to look about on his own and see if he could find the right place where they kept the old newspapers. He looked for a few minutes and realized that he could not make a bit of sense out of the filing system. "Maybe I'll ask one of the students," he thought. But, they all seemed so engrossed in their reading he did not want to disturb any of them.

"Just ask the librarian, Stupid," he chided himself, "She's hired to help. I'll just wait till she's off the phone."

He pretended to look at some of the recent papers that were spread on the table closest to the librarian's desk. He was listening for her phone conversation to end, but did not want to seem impatient or to interrupt. When she completed the conversation and hung up the phone, Jamie approached her and in his meekest voice said, "Excuse me, I don't know exactly where to look for an old newspaper, could you . . ."

The librarian interrupted him before he could finish his question, "Can't you see I'm on break?!" she said as she turned and walked toward a door leading to a back room.

Humiliated and angry, Jamie ran down the four flights of stairs and out onto the campus. He turned to look at the building he had just left and muttered to himself, "What is this, be rude to Jamie day?"

"Did I say or do something wrong?" he wondered. "There must be a way to get these people to help you without first biting your head off."

Name _____ Date _____

CASE ANALYSIS WORKSHEET

Bureaucracy

What is this case about? Immerse yourself in this case by assuming the position of Jamie Huston who is trying to get help from librarians without success.

Get the facts. List the facts that you know about Jamie and his predicament:

1. _____

2. _____

3. _____

4. _____

5. _____

State the problem, issue or question that needs to be resolved.

_____

_____

List several ways that the problem might be resolved.

1. _____

2. _____

3. _____

Write down the best way to solve the problem and why you would solve it that way.

_____

_____

_____

_____

CHAPTER 6: Campus Safety

Safety on campus needs to be taken seriously. We do not like to think about crimes being committed on college campuses, but to learn ahead of time how to keep safe and avoid being a victim of crime is well worth the effort.

■ Strange Glances

This is a case of a first-year college student who is sexually assaulted while doing research in the campus library on a Sunday afternoon. She escapes physical harm, but emerges from the library feeling disgusted, violated and fearful. She wonders what she should do next.

■ The Midnight Errand

Abby Vincent wanted to get involved in campus life early in her first semester. When she did not get a bid from the sorority she rushed, she decided to run for president of her residence hall. It was midnight on the eve of the first day of campaigning and she wanted to get started on her campaign posters. She remembered the "open 24 hours" sign on a Revco store near campus and thought about going there to get poster materials.

Her car was parked several blocks away in a campus parking garage that was not well lighted. She recalled the warnings of her father and university staff about campus safety as she wondered what to do.

■ The Stranger

Ben Jones woke up in his room in the residence hall to find a stranger going through his wallet. The stranger ran out of the room when he realized that Ben had awakened. Still groggy, Ben followed him to the door and saw him duck into a room down the hall.

■ Shaving Cream Initiations

This case revolved around initiation practices at a small, church-affiliated college in the Southeast. A concerned residence hall director, Betsy, discovers what she considered to be acts of hazing and is struggling with how to respond.

■ The Chat Room

This case is about Bridget Spencer who, early in her freshman year at Midstate University, becomes hooked on the Internet and escapes into chat rooms where she "meets" a man and eventually gives him her phone number. The man begins to call to try to recruit her to perform in a porn movie. She is now afraid to answer the phone and fears that the man might come to campus looking for her.

Suggested Reading

Ellis, D. (1997). *Becoming a Master Student.* Boston, MA: Houghton Mifflin Company. Chapter 10.

CASE STUDY

Strange Glances

(This case study was prepared in cooperation with Paige Wilbanks, Assistant Director of Student Development and Coordinator of Volunteer Services at Wake Forest University. It is intended solely to initiate class discussion. All names and some peripheral facts have been disguised.)

The main floor of Walker Benefield Library was busy as usual. Students were checking out books, working with the on-line catalog system at computer terminals, and making copies of needed materials—a typical scene for a Sunday afternoon. Karen Simpson somehow did not feel part of the activity. She stood fearfully alone in the door of the elevator, overwhelmed with the feelings of dismay.

Karen Simpson

Karen had been at the University of Summerville for only two weeks. She had already established many new friendships in the residence hall and had begun to feel as much at home on this urban campus of 26,000 students as a new freshman could.

Karen was determined to be a success at the university. The odds, though, were somewhat against her. She was a provisionally admitted student, and was the first in her family to go to college. Despite these factors, she was driven to make her mother proud. Her mother, a single parent, had impressed upon her the importance of a college education and encouraged Karen to make something of herself. Though she missed her family, especially her four-year old sister, she had not yet gone back home to visit even though home was only a short hour and a half away. She wanted to make the most of this college experience and enjoyed spending time with new friends on the weekends.

Even this early into her freshman year, Karen already was feeling the academic pressures of university life. Her provisional admission status required that she take a full load of courses and earn at least a 2.0 grade point average to remain at the university after her freshman year.

The Library

On Sunday afternoon she headed to the library for an early start on the freshman seminar research paper. She began her work going through the computerized card catalog in one of the carrels on the main floor. It was there that she noticed a man staring at her. He was dressed in baggy khaki pants, running shoes, and an untucked T-shirt. Karen was struck by his glances and wondered if he might be in one of her classes or if she had met him somewhere else on campus. Unsure of whether he even recognized her as someone he thought he knew, Karen continued her research.

After about 45 minutes in the carrel, Karen realized she needed to begin locating the resources she had identified in her computer search. It was already 5:15 and she wanted to finish her work at the library before dark. She and her hallmate, Sherry, had agreed to meet on the main floor at 6:30 and walk back across campus to the residence hall.

The Stranger

When Karen reached the third floor of the library, she noticed the absence of students and staff on that floor. "At least it will be quiet," she thought to herself.

After locating the books she had identified in her search, she nestled into an isolated study carrel in the back corner of the large room and began reading. Within five minutes she glanced up to see that same man staring at her again, as he had done on the main floor.

This time Karen felt uncomfortable and scanned the room for other students or staff. "Who is this guy?" she wondered to herself. Seeing no one, she considered leaving. But she felt silly being scared over something as simple as a guy's glance. "After all, I'm in the university library, not some alleyway," she told herself. With this thought to convince her, she continued her reading.

Within a few minutes, Karen looked up to see herself face to face with the stranger. He stood boldly beside her study carrel, only his shoulders and head were visible to her over the carrel. He began asking her questions.

"I can't take my eyes off you, what's your name?"

His forwardness made her very uncomfortable, but he remained partly hidden behind the carrel. She told him her name and asked for his. He remained silent. His eyes were intense as he looked her up and down. With only a moment's hesitation, Karen stood up to leave and saw that he was ejaculating behind the carrel.

Disgusted, violated, and fearful, she wove her way through the stacks toward the elevator. He followed close behind. She slammed her hand against the elevator button and the doors opened. "What a break," she thought. Usually you had to wait a few minutes for the elevator to get to your floor. But, today she was lucky. Before he reached the elevator, she had frantically pressed the button for the main floor and the doors had closed, leaving her alone for the ride.

When she reached the main floor, the doors slowly opened. She hesitantly stepped off the elevator. She saw no sign of the strange man. As a matter of fact, nothing seemed unusual. Straight ahead, students were busy researching on the computers and others chatted with friends. Everything looked the same as it had when she had left just a short while before. But, for her, the world had changed. She stood for a moment looking out over the scene and wondering what she should do next.

Name _____ Date _____

CASE ANALYSIS WORKSHEET

Strange Glances

What is this case about?　　This case calls for you to put yourself in Karen Simpson's place as a freshman who has just experienced a sexual assault as she was doing her library research.

Get the facts.　　List the facts that you know about Karen and this incident:

1. _____

2. _____

3. _____

4. _____

5. _____

State the problem, issue or question that needs to be resolved.

_____

_____

List several ways that the problem might be resolved.

1. _____

2. _____

3. _____

Write down the best way to solve the problem and why you would solve it that way.

_____

_____

_____

_____

CASE STUDY

The Midnight Errand

(This case study was prepared in cooperation with Tammy Ott, Director of Academic Services at Coastal Carolina University, Conway, South Carolina. It is intended solely to initiate class discussion. All names and some peripheral facts have been disguised.)

Abigail Vincent had been thinking all evening about running for president of her residence hall government. It was now about midnight and she decided she had done enough thinking. If she was going to run, it was time to do something about it.

Abby, as everyone called her, turned 18 during the summer and was now a new freshman in her second week at Southern University. It had been a disappointing week. She had gone through sorority rush but did not get a bid from the sorority she wanted most. That was the last thing she expected. Rejection was not something with which she had much experience. In high school she had been one of the most popular students. Attractive and full of life, she had been selected as a cheerleader and invited to join Debs, an exclusive college-like sorority. She had lots of friends and lots of fun.

Abby's decision to run for president was a last minute decision. The campaign started tomorrow and she wanted to get her posters up first thing in the morning. That was the way Abby always did things; wait until the last possible moment.

She had an excuse. Two years ago she was tested and found to have a problem focusing her attention. They called it "attention deficit disorder." It had an effect on her grades in high school and she had just barely gotten into the university. As it was, she had been admitted on probation and would have to get at least a 2.0 grade point average in her freshman courses to keep from being academically dismissed. Medication had helped get the problem under control, but old habits die hard and waiting until the last moment was a habit she had not overcome.

When she told Lynette Womack, her roommate, that she was going to run for president, Lynette wasn't at all surprised. They had been best friends in high school and had decided to go to the same university so they could be roommates. Lynette loved the way Abby always said exactly what was on her mind. No one ever had to guess what she was thinking; she just never had an unspoken thought. Lynette had gotten used to Abby's impulsive way of doing things and her quickly changing moods. So, the sudden excitement about running for president after the disappointment of not getting into the sorority was not surprising.

Abby got right to work designing campaign flyers and posters to put on bulletin boards throughout the residence hall. Lynette made a suggestion or two, but her energy level was no match for Abby's and she thought she had better go to bed and get some rest.

CHAPTER SIX

In what seemed like a matter of minutes, Abby finished her designs and began thinking about what to do next. She needed to get bright fluorescent-colored paper for her flyers and poster board with colored markers for her posters. She wanted to make enough posters for each floor of the three-storied residence hall and enough copies of her flyer to slip one under the door of each resident.

The campus bookstore was closed at this hour, but the university was located in the downtown area and she remembered seeing several drug stores close by campus as she drove around the neighborhood on her several "runs" to the grocery store. One of the Revco stores had a red neon sign in the window that said, "Open 24 hours." She couldn't remember exactly where it was, but she knew it was fairly close and she could find it if she had to.

The parking garage where Abby parked her car was about four blocks from her room. It was one of those creepy places; a typical concrete structure where footsteps echoed in what always seemed like semi-darkness even in the middle of the day. The university used to have a security guard posted at the garage to prevent vandalism and help students feel safe. Budget cuts, however, had reduced the security force and the garage was one place where guards were no longer stationed.

The warnings she had heard from school officials and residence hall staff about safety on campus popped into her head and she could hear her father saying, "Be careful. That's a large campus down there and nobody's going to be there to watch out for you. It's all in your hands. Don't take chances." She felt for her keys and the mace that was attached to the chain. "Should I?" she thought.

Name _____ Date _____

CASE ANALYSIS WORKSHEET

The Midnight Errand

What is this case about? Imagine yourself in Abby Vincent's place as she tries to decide whether she should walk several blocks alone across campus to her car. It is midnight, but she wants to get started on a project and needs to go to an all-night store for supplies.

Get the facts. List the facts that you know about Abby and her predicament:

1. _____
2. _____
3. _____
4. _____
5. _____

State the problem, issue or question that needs to be resolved.

_____
_____

List several ways that the problem might be resolved.

1. _____
2. _____
3. _____

Write down the best way to solve the problem and why you would solve it that way.

_____
_____
_____

CASE STUDY

The Stranger

(This case study was prepared in cooperation with Scott Ranges, at the University of South Carolina. It is intended solely to initiate class discussion. All names and some peripheral facts have been disguised.)

At 5:30 am, the bright hallway light shone into Ben's room and startled him awake. "My door shouldn't be open," he thought to himself. Out of the corner of his eye he saw a figure and realized he wasn't alone. Standing at the foot of his bed was a stranger fumbling through Ben's wallet. "What's he doing here?" Ben thought to himself. At that moment, the stranger realized Ben was awake and ran past him out of the room.

Ben Jones grew up in a large city. As a kid, he was somewhat of a bully and troublemaker. But, when he reached high school he put that behind him and "cleaned up his act." He enjoyed his high school experience and was very active. He played a number of sports and participated in various activities. He was successful enough with his studies to be accepted to the largest university in the state, which was located in his own city. He thought bigger was better and had looked forward to starting college.

To take full advantage of his college experience, Ben decided to live on campus. He shared a room with one of his friends from high school. His classes turned out to be enjoyable and he found himself making friends with people he met in classes and in his residence hall. College was turning out to be everything he had hoped and he was having a great time, until the morning he awoke to find a stranger in his room.

Like many college dorms, Ben's room was a double. Somehow he and his roommate managed to cram all of their stuff into the pint-sized room. Their heads rested by the hallway wall, so a lot of noise could be heard on party nights. Ben and his roommate each put their dressers at the foot of their beds, and pushed their desks against the far wall. Both were good about locking the door, but on this night, Ben's roommate had been writing a paper and had forgotten to lock the door.

At 5:30 am, Ben noticed the light from the hall shining in his room. He knew something was strange, but it was not until he saw the figure standing at the foot of his bed that Ben realized what was happening. The figure had a stocky build and wore a bandanna over his face and a baseball cap. He was startled when he realized that Ben had awakened. He made a comment that Ben did not quite understand. Still, groggy, Ben realized the stranger had his wallet and he began to get up. Before he had time to react, the stranger ran out of the room. Ben followed him to the door and saw him duck into room 245, just down the hall.

Name _____   Date _____

CASE ANALYSIS WORKSHEET

The Stranger

What is this case about?   Immerse yourself in this case by putting yourself in Ben Jones' room as he awakes to see a stranger going through his wallet.

Get the facts.   List the facts that you know about Ben and his situation:

1. _____
2. _____
3. _____
4. _____
5. _____

State the problem, issue or question that needs to be resolved.

_____
_____

List several ways that the problem might be resolved.

1. _____
2. _____
3. _____

Write down the best way to solve the problem and why you would solve it that way.

_____
_____
_____
_____

CASE STUDY

Shaving Cream Initiations

(This case study was prepared in cooperation with Rebecca Bowers, Residence Hall Director at Tulane University. It is intended solely to initiate class discussion. All names and some peripheral facts have been disguised.)

"Totally crazy" was how the class described the final event of freshman orientation. It happened at the very end of an afternoon of activities that had new frosh tossing eggs, throwing water balloons and running all kinds of relay races; fun stuff that helps freshmen get to know each other. The closing activity, though, sounded a lot like hazing to Betsy Walker.

Betsy Walker was director of Bridwell Residence Hall at Rockbridge College. She had been at the college for a year, but had not gotten involved in the orientation program. For her part, she preferred to teach a section of COLL 101, a semester-long course modeled on the University 101 program developed at the University of South Carolina. Betsy felt it was important to help freshmen make a successful transition to college life and take full advantage of what Rockbridge had to offer. COLL 101 gave her a chance to relate to students on a more substantive level than was possible in a two-day freshman orientation program.

Rockbridge College

Rockbridge College was a church-related institution founded by a group of ministers in the later part of the nineteenth century. Located in a small southern town, the college enjoyed a family-like atmosphere on a campus of softly rolling hills shaded by ancient oak trees. Its enrollment of only 1,400 students made it a size where faculty and staff could come to know and care about every student. This was clear in its purpose statement which said the college intended ". . . to develop the mental, physical, moral and spiritual capacities of each student in preparation for a lifetime of personal and vocational fulfillment and responsible contribution to our democratic society."

Orientation

Somehow the topic of orientation had come up in class and Betsy had asked the students to describe their experiences at the field day activity. "Totally crazy, people were running around and screaming," said one student who told how upperclassmen, serving as orientation leaders, had attacked the freshmen with shaving cream.

"Attacked?" Betsy asked, trying to draw him out.

"Well, as soon as we walked out of the gym door, the orientation leaders started to spray everyone with shaving cream. And when they thought someone was covered enough, they hosed them down with water."

"Did anyone get hurt?" Betsy asked.

"One girl got shaving cream in her eye under her contact lens," said one student.

Another told of seeing someone fall and scrape his knee.

Betsy wanted to know more and asked if any of the freshmen were given cans of shaving cream to spray back at the upperclassmen. They responded, "Only if we took it away from one of the orientation staff."

Betsy wondered if this type of activity might not be getting pretty close to hazing. The students seemed to think it was part of the school's tradition, so she let it drop and moved on to other topics.

Early the following week, Heather burst through the door of Bridwell covered from head to foot with shaving cream. Betsy was in the front hallway and could not help smiling; Heather looked like a little storm cloud. "What happened to you?" she asked.

Heather said, "I was just initiated onto the women's soccer team."

"That's odd," thought Betsy. Heather had a partial scholarship and had been on campus for three weeks already practicing with the soccer team. Why would she just now be "initiated"?

"Tell me about it," Betsy urged.

"Well, all the first-year soccer players went on a scavenger hunt in the men's dorms and when we were done, the other players sprayed us with shaving cream," was Heather's brief reply. "Can I go wash this stuff off?" she asked as she ran toward her room.

Hazing

Betsy was vaguely uncomfortable with what she had seen. This "tradition" of shave creaming the first-year students could easily be seen as a hazing ritual. She knew there were regulations for Greek organizations on campus that strictly forbade any type of hazing for their members. She also remembered seeing something in the student handbook about hazing and harassment. She decided to look it up again to see exactly what it said.

The handbook indicated that all students were required to sign the Honor Code and follow the Code of Conduct. The conduct code included this definition of hazing:

> *... any action taken or any situation created, whether on or off campus, to produce intentional mental or physical discomfort, embarrassment, harassment or ridicule.*

The Code said "no" to hazing, but the practice on campus seemed to say something else.

The Problem

Concerned, Betsy turned to one of her colleagues, another hall director, Barney Lucas. She asked him what he thought about the shaving cream incidents. Barney wasn't surprised. He had been told by a freshman in his hall that the same thing had happened with the football team. This worried him, he said, because he had heard that one of the neighboring colleges was being threatened with a lawsuit from the family of a freshman football player who claimed he had been hazed.

The story from the other college was that four football players, all upperclassmen, came to a freshman's room one evening and accused him of breaking curfew the night before. He denied it, but was forced to submit to a beating on his bare legs and buttocks. The players used belts and rubber shower shoes and left bruises. He was not the only freshman this happened to. That same evening upperclassmen cornered and "spanked" as many freshmen players as they could get their hands on. The freshmen were told that was what happened to smart-aleck freshmen who disrespected upperclassmen.

Both Betsy and Barney knew that hazing was illegal in their state. The state Legislature passed a hazing law in 1993 which allowed for penalties of up to a $500 fine or up to 12 months' imprisonment, or both.

As she and Barney talked, she came to realize that he had the same hesitancy about bringing up the Rockbridge incidents to their boss that she had. Their boss, the Dean of Students, had graduated from Rockbridge and had worked at the college for over 30 years. He loved his alma mater and spent a great deal of time after hours and weekends on campus interacting with students. He was proud of the college and its traditions. As a matter of fact, he himself was seen by students and many of the alumni as one of the "traditions" on campus.

Betsy had a very uneasy feeling about particular traditions that seemed to promote hazing and harassment. It might have been alright in the "good ole days" when such treatment was considered a rite of passage. But, things were different now.

With a conviction that she had to do something, she set out across campus to speak to the Dean. As she walked she wondered how she would approach him and what she would say.

Name _____ Date _____

CASE ANALYSIS WORKSHEET

Shaving Cream Initiations

What is this case about? Betsy Walker is a residence director who becomes aware of a campus practice that she thinks might be hazing. Put yourself in Betsy's place and see how you might react.

Get the facts. List the facts that you know about Betsy's predicament:

1. _____
2. _____
3. _____
4. _____
5. _____

State the problem, issue or question that needs to be resolved.

_____

_____

List several ways that the problem might be resolved.

1. _____
2. _____
3. _____

Write down the best way to solve the problem and why you would solve it that way.

_____

_____

_____

_____

CASE STUDY

The Chat Room

(This case study was prepared in cooperation with Dr. Craig Stephenson, Assistant Resident Dean at the University of California at San Diego. It is intended solely to initiate class discussion. All names and some peripheral facts have been disguised.)

Bridget Spencer was more addicted to the Internet than she thought she should be. As she sat locked in her dorm room, she knew that things had gone too far. "That guy in the chat room seemed nice enough," she thought, "how could I be so stupid to give him my number?"

Bridget did not have a computer of her own, but she wanted to learn how to use one. As a matter of fact, she had registered for University 101, Freshman Seminar, because in that course students learned how to use the Internet and got their own e-mail accounts. Her interest grew rapidly after her first three weeks in college.

During those weeks, Bridget was side-tracked by the party scene at Midstate University and her college career had gotten off to a rocky start. Too many parties led her to miss some of her classes and soon she found herself exhausted, disillusioned and disinterested. She wanted out and found an escape in computers. There she sought intellectual conversation and an opportunity to meet new and interesting people. One of her University 101 classmates, James Hillman, fueled her interest by introducing her to chat rooms on the Internet.

The chat rooms offered Bridget what she was looking for in her search for a new outlet at college; the opportunity to meet different people, to learn different cultures, to compare different ideas and to voice her own opinion. This was something the party scene could never offer her, "Because," as Bridget put it, "everyone else is too smashed to understand what you are saying."

This new world of chat rooms also offered Bridget relative anonymity which diminished her fear of being rejected because of how she looked. Her short, shiny black hair and long baggy pants and boots had brought taunts about her sexual orientation from some people in the past and had distracted them from getting to know the real Bridget. Equally important to her was the belief that chatting on the Internet was not half as hazardous as attending a party where somebody might put "roofies" in her drink and she would not remember what happened after that. "It was a way of keeping out of trouble," she liked to say.

For someone seeking relief from the boredom of television, parties and the opportunity to fill the time that her 12 credit hours of study did not fill, the chat room seemed the ideal environment in which to learn and have fun. It provided diversity (chatting to people of all ages, cultures and lifestyles), stimulation, stress relief and above all, a sense of security that she was out of harm's way, safe in the bowels of the university library. Three to four hours a day were spent in various chat rooms; "going off on somebody," "making someone else happy," "giving advice," and generally, "being cheered up." Once, she spent the whole night on the computer; when the library closed at midnight, she went to the engineering computer lab where she got on the computer until 9:00 am the next morning.

It was in one such chat room, "Hot Tub," that she first met "Percular," after using the handle, "Sheba, the Love Goddess" (she thought it fit her image in high school as a romantic, gypsy type). Percular seemed really nice and gave no indication that his intentions were anything but honorable, making only basic inquiries about her interests and hobbies, what she did at college and inquiring how her day had been. Bridget was aware that a lot of individuals on the 'Net indulged in "cyber sex," particularly those in the "Hot Tub," but he did not appear to be one of them. He told her that he was 25 years old, from Virginia, interested in rock concerts and reading and that he considered himself a romantic, all in all, she thought, "a pretty cool guy."

She explained it this way, "He never acted interested in cyber sex or anything, so I was thinking he was not a creep. About three weeks after I first communicated with him, and feeling comfortable about it, I sent him my telephone number. Then, he comes on the telephone . . ."

During the first telephone conversation, she remembered that he, "dilly dallied for a while, chatted about things in general and was very polite. Then he just said, 'Well, I'm in this network and we are very sexually oriented and we would like for you to think about joining our network and being a movie star.'" The movie, he explained, was to be about a lonely college girl who meets this guy in a bar and leaves with him, after which "stuff happens."

Then it clicked, "This is a porn movie and he is trying to recruit me!"

She mumbled something about him joking. He was perfectly serious she soon learned, and she abruptly ended the conversation.

He persisted with his calls. "They came at really inconvenient times," she recalled, "like seven in the morning or just when I was leaving for class." The number of calls increased and each time he pleaded with her to reconsider joining the network. Soon, Bridget was afraid to pick up the phone or to go out of her room, "just in case he came down," she remembered.

Blaming herself, Bridget wondered what this guy might do next. Frustrated and fearful, she wished her phone would never again ring and wondered what she might do to stop his harassing calls.

Name _____ Date _____

CASE ANALYSIS WORKSHEET
The Chat Room

What is this case about?   Immerse yourself in this case by placing yourself in Bridget Spencer's shoes. You have met a man on the Internet that is now calling you to perform in a porn movie. How can you deal with him?

Get the facts.   List the facts that you know about Bridget and the situation:

1. _____

2. _____

3. _____

4. _____

5. _____

State the problem, issue or question that needs to be resolved.

_____

_____

List several ways that the problem might be resolved.

1. _____

2. _____

3. _____

Write down the best way to solve the problem and why you would solve it that way.

_____

_____

_____

_____

CHAPTER 7

Academic Integrity

A fundamental principal of academic life is intellectual honesty. Each of us should set the highest standards of honesty for ourselves. Academic integrity also means that we gain a deep understanding of our chosen major and develop the competence to evaluate our own knowledge in that subject area. In other words, we should develop the ability to think independently.

Taking responsibility for our own learning is probably the most difficult and most satisfying experience of our academic life.

■ When the Music Stops

Amy Burkhalter played the flute since childhood and chose music as her major in college. However, she injured her wrist during the summer before college and could no longer play the flute. The faculty in the School of Music told her she must play an instrument in order to major in music and, with her injury and inability to play the flute, she could no longer major in music. Disappointed, she wondered what she could do.

■ Keeping the Scholarship

In this case, Frank, a commuter student, feels the pressure of a crowded schedule and sees his grades beginning to fall. He worried about keeping his scholarship and wondered what else he might do to turn things around.

■ A Golden Opportunity

Katie Sutton's chemistry quiz was her first test as a college freshman. She wanted to do well but had not gotten as much time to study as she would have liked. Later, the professor handed back her test ungraded and asked that she re-do the answer sheet because she did it wrong the first time. A couple of answers were wrong and she saw an opportunity to change them without the professor knowing.

■ This Paper Is Plagiarized

This case depicts a freshman, Amy Sloan, being accused of plagiarism by her instructor. She is not sure how to respond. Her paper is included as an exhibit with this case.

■ Signing the Honor Code

Robert Cline had been warned by his older brother not to sign anything. His brother had gotten into trouble when he signed up for a credit card without his parents' knowledge and had run up a large debt that took five years to pay off. Now, Robert was being asked to sign the Honor Code and he was hesitant.

Suggested Readings

Salane, L. B. (1997). "Choosing a major and planning a career." In Gardner, J. N., & Jewler, A. J. *Your College Experience: Strategies for Success.* Belmont, CA: Wadsworth Publishing Company.

Ritter, D. A. (1997). "Academic integrity: Honesty in the classroom." In Gardner, J. N., & Jewler, A. J. *Your College Experience: Strategies for Success.* Belmont, CA: Wadsworth Publishing Company.

CASE STUDY

When the Music Stops

(This case study was prepared in cooperation with Nina Long Glisson, Conference Coordinator, National Resource Center for the First-Year Experience and Students in Transition at the University of South Carolina. It is intended solely to initiate class discussion. All names and some peripheral facts have been disguised.)

Playing the flute was all Amy Burkhalter ever wanted to do with her life. She had played the flute since she was a small child and now, as she began her college career, she had no other desire than to continue what she loved, so she chose music as her major. The school of music thought otherwise. The faculty had asked her to seek another major outside of music. She was stunned when she heard the decision and scrambled to make sense of its meaning.

Amy had spent most of her life in Michigan, where her family raised show horses. Then, four years ago, she moved with her mother and older sister to Gaffney, South Carolina. Her sister was an accomplished horseback rider and had several championships to her name. Amy was every bit as good in her own way; playing the flute. The flute was Amy's way of competing with her sister and she had worked hard enough at it to earn a partial scholarship in music to the university whose flute program was recognized as one of the very best in the country.

The move to South Carolina had been very difficult for both Amy and her sister. There were no horses there and her sister had to give up riding. The family started raising and training show dogs, but Amy hated it and was never happy in Gaffney. Small-town life just did not suit her. She wished the family would move back to Michigan.

Last summer while rollerblading, Amy slipped and tried to catch herself with her hands as she fell. When the palm of her left hand hit the pavement, she heard a sickening crunch as delicate bones in her wrist shattered. Eight weeks in a cast had been almost unbearable. The cast had prevented her from practicing or playing her flute; the wrist would not bend enough to allow her fingers to reach the keys. When the cast came off, she immediately picked up her flute and began to practice. In the following weeks she spent several hours each day with the flute trying to get back into form. Her wrist did not respond quickly. It was stiff and she often found it painful to move her fingers, especially toward the end of her practice session. When she told her physician about the pain, she examined the wrist and fingers and determined that the injury had left Amy with tendinitis and carpel tunnel syndrome. "It will only get worse and we can't do anything to reverse it," the physician had advised. Amy was crushed.

When she got to the university, Amy had resigned herself to the fact that she may never be able to play the flute professionally. "But," she reasoned, "I can always teach music." When she discussed her situation with the people in the school of music she was told she could not major in music, not even music education, if she could not play an instrument.

Alone in her room, she tearfully thought about what she would do next.

Name _____ Date _____

CASE ANALYSIS WORKSHEET

When the Music Stops

What is this case about? Experience Amy Burkhalter's disappointment when she is told that she cannot major in music because of an injury to her wrist. Now she wonders what she can do.

Get the facts. List the facts that you know about Amy and her situation:

1. _____
2. _____
3. _____
4. _____
5. _____

State the problem, issue or question that needs to be resolved.

_____

_____

List several ways that the problem might be resolved.

1. _____
2. _____
3. _____

Write down the best way to solve the problem and why you would solve it that way.

_____

_____

_____

_____

CASE STUDY

Keeping the Scholarship

(This case study was prepared in cooperation with Dan Rodkin, Area Director at the University of Tampa, and Shannon Fennell, Assistant Director of Career Services at Stetson University. It is intended solely to initiate class discussion. All names and some peripheral facts have been disguised.)

"Boy, this ride gets longer and longer every day," Frank thought as he drove the unscenic, thirty-minute trek home after marching band practice. Driving to and from Central State University stole an hour from a day already filled with classes, band practice and music lessons.

"When am I supposed to find time to study?" he wondered.

At least the ride gave him the chance to think and be alone. When he got home, he knew he would be met with his parent's questions about school, band and everything else.

Grades

Frank did not want his parents to know yet that his grades this first semester at CSU were suffering. His parents would wonder why, after making straight As in high school, was he now only managing to make C pluses. Was it because he wasn't studying enough? He was studying so much more than he did a year ago. Perhaps it had something to do with the fact that his adviser convinced him to take seventeen hours of classes. "Damn!" he thought, "if I'd only known a couple of months ago how tough it would be to balance that many classes with band practice and music lessons." Now it was too late to drop any courses from his load. He'd have to tough it out.

Schedule

Because music lessons two days a week and marching practice four days a week were required for his full-ride scholarship, Frank knew he could not do much to change his weekly schedule. He was not even majoring in music and yet it seemed to consume all his time. Though he did love playing his trumpet, Frank believed majoring in criminal justice was more practical than majoring in music.

When his family moved from Texas to Tennessee six months ago, Frank had left behind his girlfriend, many friends who knew about and understood his Puerto Rican roots, and his comfort zone. He thought once he started college, life could only get better. But, he still did not feel at home here despite having made several friends in classes and the marching band. The atmosphere was different; and Frank had decided that he did not like it.

The Problem

Frank did not like the feeling of defeat. He knew he was as smart as the other students at this university. Why did it seem like they had plenty of free time to hang out, while he was always worrying about something: grades, practice, pleasing his parents, keeping his scholarship?

"What else can I try?" he wondered. He had studied several different ways. He made note cards to help him. He had even recorded himself reading and played the tapes back during his trips to and from school. Obviously none of this was doing the trick. He had thought about talking to his professors; but he just knew that would not do any good, considering he was only one of a couple hundred students in several of his classes. Maybe this was what it meant to be a freshman; being overwhelmed and losing confidence. "Am I the only one who feels this way?" he wondered. "Is there anyone who can help?"

As he pulled into the driveway at home, Frank tried to think of a new response for his parent's inquiries about the day and his classes.

Name _____ Date _____

CASE ANALYSIS WORKSHEET

Keeping the Scholarship

What is this case about?   Put yourself in Frank's position and feel the time pressures and falling grades. How can this situation be turned around?

Get the facts.   List the facts that you know about Frank and his predicament:

1. _____
2. _____
3. _____
4. _____
5. _____

State the problem, issue or question that needs to be resolved.

_____

_____

List several ways that the problem might be resolved.

1. _____
2. _____
3. _____

Write down the best way to solve the problem and why you would solve it that way.

_____

_____

_____

_____

CASE STUDY

A Golden Opportunity

(This case study was prepared in cooperation with Cecily Crow, Director of Student Activities at Greensboro College. It is intended solely to initiate class discussion. All names and some peripheral facts have been disguised.)

Katie Sutton sat uncomfortably at her desk. In front of her lay the chemistry exam her professor had just put there. He wanted her to go back over it and fix how she had recorded her answers. It was a multiple-choice and short answer exam and she had mistakenly circled her answers instead of putting the letter of the correct answer in the blanks provided. "Wow," she thought, "a golden opportunity to change some answers!"

Going to College

Katie had moved many times during her childhood and adolescence. Her father was a railroad worker and was frequently transferred from place to place as his career advanced. Her family was living in southern Georgia when she graduated from high school and it was not long before they moved to North Carolina. She moved with them and began working as a teacher's aide in an elementary school. At the end of her first year, her father was again transferred.

Katie again moved, but this time she decided to go to college instead of trying to find another job. She visited the university located in her family's new home town and liked what she saw. Soon she had gained admission and shortly thereafter began attending classes. All the while she continued to live at home.

Katie was not ready for the amount of work that she found in college. In fact, she felt high school may not have adequately prepared her for college-level work. She had been an A student in high school and graduated 22nd in her class of 250. She was motivated to work hard and her parents and teachers had instilled in her a strong sense of Christian values. Now that she was in college, her confidence fell. She was enrolled in several large lecture classes and found the professors to be, as she put it, "not very personal." She worried that her success in college would never measure up to her accomplishments in high school.

Chemistry Class

One of her large classes was chemistry. The professor scheduled five exams throughout the semester and they accounted for 75 percent of the final grade. Her first test in college was in this class and she did not begin preparing for it until the night before. Her anxiety level was pretty high when she started the test, but by the time she finished both the multiple choice and short answer sections of the test, she began to feel her confidence return and thought she would get a good grade.

The Returned Test

A week later, Katie received her test back. On it was a note that read, "Not graded—see me." Katie walked immediately to the front of the lecture hall to talk to her professor. He said that she had circled her answers instead of writing them in the blanks provided. So, for him to accurately grade the exam, she would need to transfer her answers to the blanks. Relieved that this was not a major task, Katie went back to her desk. When she sat down, she opened the test to discover that her professor had already graded the first eight questions and she had gotten two of them wrong. Then, the thought struck her, "a golden opportunity!" If she changed the two wrong answers when she transferred her work, she would gain more points on the test. Who would know?

In high school, answer swapping was common and no one ever got expelled for cheating. But, this was college. Were students expelled from college for this? What would happen if she were caught? The class was so large that the professor would probably never notice the changes. Thoughts raced through her mind and her heart pounded as she sat stiffly in her chair.

Name _____ Date _____

CASE ANALYSIS WORKSHEET

A Golden Opportunity

What is this case about? Place yourself in Katie Sutton's position. You can help yourself to a better grade on the first chemistry test without anyone knowing.

Get the facts. List the facts that you know about Katie and her situation:

1. _____
2. _____
3. _____
4. _____
5. _____

State the problem, issue or question that needs to be resolved.

_____
_____

List several ways that the problem might be resolved.

1. _____
2. _____
3. _____

Write down the best way to solve the problem and why you would solve it that way.

_____
_____
_____
_____

CASE STUDY

This Paper Is Plagiarized

(This case study was prepared in cooperation with Jennifer Moye Lisznyai, Human Resources at Richland Memorial Hospital. It is intended solely to initiate class discussion. All names and some peripheral facts have been disguised.)

Amy Sloan could not believe what she was hearing. Her instructor, John Bell, had asked her to see him after class and now, as she stood in front of him near the classroom door, he handed her the paper she had turned in last week. She flipped the pages quickly and saw no marks, not even a grade. When she looked up, she heard him say, "This paper is plagiarized."

This was Amy's first semester as a college freshman and it had not been an easy start to college. Her family lived in a rather small town nearly an hour and a half distant. Her leaving home for the first time had not been easy for her mother. As a matter of fact, her mother had called several times in a state of near hysteria and Amy had responded by driving home to be with her and to help reassure her that everything was alright at college; she was still alive and healthy.

By going home, Amy had missed five class meetings of her freshman seminar course. She did not want her frequent absences to be a problem for her, so she had met with Mr. Bell and confided that she had a personal problem at home and had to be there on several days which had caused her to miss class. She showed him her journal, which was required for the course, and let him see that she had faithfully continued to write her journal entries even though she had not been in class. He seemed to understand.

The assignment required that students pick a topic and write a research paper using at least four sources of reference. Each student was also to give an oral report to the class on the research paper they had done. Amy decided to write about schizophrenia since she had done a lot of reading about that subject and knew quite a bit about it.

This was Amy's first college paper, so she did not know exactly what to expect. She liked to write and had been encouraged by her high school teachers who often told her that she was a good writer. That encouragement had led her to experiment with her writing and she had done some poetry and short stories. She felt comfortable and successful with her writing and had chosen English as her major.

And now she listened in shock as Mr. Bell continued, "It's not a regular research paper, you couldn't have written it. No freshman could write this kind of paper!"

She looked back down at her paper (Exhibit 1), and, with a rising sense of panic, she searched for the right words with which to explain.

EXHIBIT 1

Schizophrenia: an overview of the disease
and one woman's struggle for sanity.
September 19, 1995

Lori Shiller was the perfect child in what seemed like the perfect family. She had loving parents and two brothers that looked up to her. she was a straight "A" student, was very involved with high school, and had a very bright future in front of her. The suburb she and her family lived in had an extremely high status and was very wealthy. At seventeen she was working as a camp counselor at Lincoln Farm Summer Camp. and it was there that she heard them for the first time. she heard something that no one else heard at the time and that no one would ever hear. "You must die! You must die! You will die!"

Not knowing what was wrong with her, she tried her hardest to keep it inside. but the rest of the camp staff started to notice a change in her always perky attitude. They noticed how spaced out she was and that she was extremely depressed. She was sent home. Her parents were on vacation at the time, so there would be no questions asked and she would have a few days to get herself together. She hid the screaming voices inside her head and went on with life as normal.

The next fall sh began her college career at Tufts University. She shared an apartment with two of her closest friends. She tried to conceal the voices even though they became more frequent and sinister. Her mood changes became violent and threatened the lives of her roommates and herself. At twenty-three she made her first suicide attempt. The was the first warning of a secret disease taking root in her mind.

Her parents were shocked at the thought of Lori being mentally ill, and kept thinking that she was just depressed and that everything would work itself out. the staff at the Payne Whitney Clinic in New York had different ideas. Lori was breaking down. Almost every person she came into contact with was showered with the voices in Lori's mind. They shouted at her, threatened her, and gave her ideas of killing everyone. The voices not only talked to her and wouldn't let her sleep at night, they occupied her every moment. Then the hallucinations began. At some moments she would look at her hands and they would be splitting open oozing blood. This type of occurrence became a normality.

Even after the doctors diagnosed Lori with chronic Schizophrenia, she still thought nothing of her illness. She found the voices irritating, but had no idea of its seriousness. Lore couldn't believe that no one heard the voices she heard. She was self conscious around others because of it. She was discharged from the hospital with the idea that she would live at home under supervision. Lori convinced the doctors that she could do it on her own. This was her parents and her doctors first mistake.

On her own, Lori attended day classes at the hospital while her parents worked. But soon she found it easy to skip the classes and began hanging out with the wrong people. She started doing cocaine because it helped smother the voices, but her habit turned into something she could not handle. Her parents began to threaten her about ending her drug habit and she had a mental relapse. She tried to commit suicide again and was forcibly hospitalized.

Lori had gained almost fifty pounds by this point, weighing in at one hundred and seventy pounds which was far from her normal, slim physique. A lot of the weight gain came from heavy medication, but depression played a key role as well. Lori had been pulled into the mental health care system and eventually was hospitalized five different times. She had many relapses, two suicide attempts, and a screaming, full-blown schizophrenia that seemed beyond the reach of any cure.

Two women, and incredible staff, a loving family, a self-examination, and a newfound will to live pulled Lori out of madness and she began to cope. Lori co-wrote her book <u>The Quiet Room</u>, she has a job on weekends, and devotes a lot of her time to mental patients and their families. But there one thing in her past that will be with her forever...The voices. (Bennett, Shiller, The Quiet Room)

Schizophrenia in a literal sense means "split mind", but the disease does not imply a split personality. It is not someone acting like two different people. Schizophrenia was not distinguished from other forms of psychosis until the twentieth century. (Achernect, 92)

Schizophrenia almost always develops before middle age. The first episode normally takes place sometime during adolescence or young adulthood and is followed by other increasingly detrimental episodes. The disease causes deterioration in a person's work, social relationships, and ability to look after himself or herself. (Wolman, 195)

The symptoms of schizophrenia are not routine and are not the same for every individual. Some common symptoms include isolation from family and friends, hallucinations, perpetual problems, sudden disturbances in movement, and odd speech and behavior. (Wolman, 198) "Being unable to control one's own thoughts, being isolated by a vision of reality all one' own, being commanded to act by disembodied voices-these are the experiences that make schizophrenia such a frightening experience." (Shiller, 278)

Scientists agree that schizophrenia has not single cause. It is the product of an interplay of biology, psychology, and culture. The disease does tend to be genetically inherited. Itis more likely to affect someone that is a close relative to a schizophrenic than the population at large. Whereas only one or two out of every one-hundred people become schizophrenic over a life time, about ten out of every one hundred children who have one schizophrenic parent eventually will develop the disorder. (Wender, 115)

Whether schizophrenia is caused by a biochemical abnormality, a neurological defect, or a bad enzyme is still open to question. Most scientists believe that the strength and severeness of the disease varies from one individual to another. (Brunner, 177)

Research has led to some breakthroughs linking a number of environmental factors to schizophrenia. For example, unclear communication within families is one potential condition, although scientists are still unsure whether miscommunication in the family is a cause of schizophrenia or an after effect. Poverty has also been associated with the disease. (Brunner, 181)

The most powerful treatment for alleviating schizophrenic symptoms is antipsychotic medication. (Horwitz, 54) These drugs have for the first time enabled patients to function without breakdowns or unpleasant symptoms. They are used to hault episodes of schizophrenia and also to prevent future problems. These drugs,however, do have drawbacks. They can produce minor side effects such as drowsiness and dry mouth and can also have long term consequences. Some patients that use the drugs for a long period of time develop a condition known as tardive dyskinesia. This disease is characterized by abnormal movements of the mouth and tongue. This is especially serious because tardive dyskinesia has no known cure and may not disappear once the patient stops using the drug. Not every patient benefits from antipsychotic drugs, and some seem not to need them at all. Some forms of psychotherapy are also used to treat schizophrenic patients. It is also used to help patients who do not receive medication. (Maisto, 97-9)

Schizophrenia is a dangerous disease that often times causes its victims to totally withdraw from society and from their normal routines. Even though in the past it was thought as only as "abnormal." or "weird", the disease known as schizophrenia is now taken seriously, and continual breakthroughs are being made to help it's victim. The disease still has not cure-only ways to lesson the symptoms and the voices. "The voices taught me about a hell that was beyond all religious beliefs, It was beyond all imagining, beyond all human hope. The voices that spoke to me were as clear and as real as any voices around me. In fact, they were more real, because they were both inside me and outside me.

"Come to me," they crooned. "Come to hell with me."

I didn't want to listen. I didn't want to hear. But I had no choice. Where would I go?" L. Shiller

Bibliography

Ackernecht, E. H. *A Short History of Psychiatry*. Hafner, 2d ed., rev., 1970.

A Casebook in Psychiatric Ethics. Brunner/Mazell, 1990.

Bennett, Amanda and Shiller, Lori. *The Quiet Room*: A Journey Out of the Torment of Madness.

Horwitz, Elinor Lander. *Madness, Magic, and Medicine*: the Treatment and Mistreatment of the Mentally Ill. Lippincott, 1977.

Maisto, Stephen A. and others. *Drug Use and Misuse*. Holt, Rinehart, and Winston, 1991.

Wender, Paul H. and Klein, Donald F. *Mind, Mood, and Medicine*: A guide to the New Biopsychiatry. Farrar, 1981.

Wolman, Benjamin B., ed. *International Encyclopedia of Psychiatry, Psychoanalysis, and Neurology*. 12v. Van Nostrand, 1977.

Name _____ Date _____

CASE ANALYSIS WORKSHEET

This Paper Is Plagiarized

What is this case about? Immerse yourself in this case by reading the paper that Amy Sloan turned in only to have her instructor say it was plagiarized. If this was your paper, how would you respond?

Get the facts. List the facts that you know about Amy and her situation:

1. _____
2. _____
3. _____
4. _____
5. _____

State the problem, issue or question that needs to be resolved.

_____

_____

List several ways that the problem might be resolved.

1. _____
2. _____
3. _____

Write down the best way to solve the problem and why you would solve it that way.

_____

_____

_____

_____

ACADEMIC INTEGRITY

CASE STUDY

Signing the Honor Code

(This case study was prepared in cooperation with Vince Roberts, Graduate Assistant at the University of South Carolina. It is intended solely to initiate class discussion. All names and some peripheral facts have been disguised.)

"Don't sign anything. It gets you in trouble."

These were the words Robert Cline remembered from his brother's story about the crushing debt he had run up after signing for a credit card during his freshman year in college. It took five years to pay it off and made the rest of his college years miserable.

Now, in his first week of college, Robert was not being asked to sign for a credit card, but he was being pressured to sign the honor code. He hesitated, mindful of his brother's "don't sign" warning.

The Honor Code

Robert was in the first week of classes and the instructor in his freshman seminar class had talked a lot about the Honor Code (see box on next page). Robert learned that the Code was a result of concerns that faculty, students and staff had about hate crimes and incivility that seemed to be growing on college campuses. It was officially adopted by the University in 1990. A bronze tablet with the text of the Code was placed in the central Quadrangle on campus, the text also appeared in many University publications, copies were mailed to new students, and framed copies hung in many campus buildings and offices. To build a tradition surrounding the code, many freshman seminar instructors required students to sign the Code during their first week in class.

Robert's Story

Robert Cline saw himself as a "reformed liar." He was not especially pleased with what he had been, but he now knew that he was better than all that. As a matter of fact, he had gained much confidence and begun to realize that he was, as he put it, "smarter than most people."

His earlier troubles had started in middle school when he had a premonition that he was going to die before the year ended. He was in eighth grade then and experienced for the first time what it meant to lose someone or something important. His dog, a pet that had been with him his whole life died. About that same time his very first girlfriend broke up with him. He was mowing the lawn when it struck him that he could actually make all the pain go away. That was when he went into the house and tried to swallow every pill in his parents medicine cabinet. They found him unconscious and got him to the hospital in time to save his life.

The Honor Code

*The community of scholars at the University
is dedicated to personal and academic excellence.*

*Choosing to join the community obligates
each member to a code of civilized behavior.*

As a student . . .

I will practice personal and academic integrity;

I will respect the dignity of all persons;

I will respect the rights and property of others;

*I will discourage bigotry, while striving to learn
from differences in people, ideal and opinions;*

*I will demonstrate concern for others, their feelings,
and their need for conditions which support
their work and development.*

*Allegiance to these ideas requires each student
to refrain from and discourage behaviors
which threaten the freedom and respect
every individual deserves.*

As a result of this incident, his parents took him to a psychiatrist for counseling. Robert soon learned that whatever he said to the psychiatrist got twisted and distorted, so he figured out what the psychiatrist wanted to hear and just lied to him. He credited the psychiatrist with turning him into a chronic and compulsive liar. For two years he lied to everyone about everything. Then, in his senior year of high school, he realized what lying was doing to him especially when his friends caught him at it. His New Year's resolution that year was to stop lying.

Robert lived in the suburbs about ten miles outside the town where the University was located. His parents wanted him to live at home, at least during his first year of college. His older brother had lived on campus and got into financial and academic trouble during his freshman year at the University. His parents were afraid the same thing would happen to Robert. So, he stayed with his parents and commuted to campus.

Robert was a business major, even though he would admit he did not look like one. He was of medium build, about five feet nine inches tall, but looked shorter with shoulders stooped from the burden he seemed to carry with him always. His hair was dark and well trimmed, but he dressed in ragged jeans and tie-dyed T-shirts not wanting the image of an up-and-coming businessman. He worked in the library shelving books to help pay a portion of his way through college.

Signing the Honor Code

Robert's brother had attended the University several years earlier and had run into trouble when he had signed up for a credit card without his parents' knowledge and ran up a debt that was beyond his ability to repay. He took a full-time job and was unable to keep up his grades. The result was that he suffered throughout his college years, never really getting to enjoy college life and always carrying the burden of debt that forced him to work full-time. Although Robert was not close to his brother, he sensed his family's frustration with the situation and came away with the message, "Don't sign anything. It gets you in trouble."

Robert was not very trusting. His experience with the psychiatrist and his brother's experience with the credit card led him to mistrust most people in authority. And, when it came to the Honor Code, he did not think anyone would uphold its requirements. "Anyone who signs it is just lying," he thought.

As his classmates were leaving class they passed by the desk and each in turn signed a poster with the Honor Code inscribed upon it. Robert was uncomfortable as he stood in the line trying to decide what he should do.

Name _____ Date _____

CASE ANALYSIS WORKSHEET

Signing the Honor Code

What is this case about?   Robert Cline is hesitant to sign the honor code. If you were in his place and had the experiences that he had, would you sign?

Get the facts.   List the facts that you know about Robert and his predicament:

1. _____
2. _____
3. _____
4. _____
5. _____

State the problem, issue or question that needs to be resolved.

_____

_____

List several ways that the problem might be resolved.

1. _____
2. _____
3. _____

Write down the best way to solve the problem and why you would solve it that way.

_____

_____

_____

_____

CHAPTER

Diversity

Meeting and getting to know people with ideas, cultures, and backgrounds that differ from our own, is the most valuable result of a college education. Fresh new ways of seeing and doing things open up to us when we allow those who differ from us the most to share in our lives.

College is rich in the diversity of people and ideas. That is why the highest levels of learning take place there, if we let it.

■ Color Lines

Yvonne Richards is a new freshman and, in her own words, describes her experience of "color lines" at her university. She is the daughter of a mixed-race marriage and has both white and black friends. She is shocked when warned not to bring her black friend to a fraternity party.

■ Southern Hospitality

Dana Parker had come from Boston to attend college in the South. She was surprised by the tolerance of racism that she encountered among her classmates. She was uncomfortable with their attitudes and wondered if she could ever adjust to her new college.

Suggested Readings

Ellis, D. (1997). *Becoming a Master Student*. Boston, MA: Houghton Mifflin Company. Chapter 7.

Rendon, L. I. (1997). "Minorities: The coming majority." In Gardner, J. N., & Jewler, A. J. *Your College Experience: Strategies*. Belmont, CA: Wadsworth Publishing Company.

Color Lines

(This case study was prepared in cooperation with Reginia Fletcher at Furman University. It is intended solely to initiate class discussion. All names and some peripheral facts have been disguised.)

Yvonne Richards grew up in the Baltimore-Washington, D.C. area, but when she left home to attend a large state university in the deep South, she was shocked. She described the experience this way:

> *To be honest, this moving experience has been a total culture shock. One of the biggest problems that I have with the atmosphere down here is the silent, yet defined color lines. It appears to me that white people stick with white people and that most black people converse with black people only. This frightened me when I got here because it isn't really like that back home. People look at me in weird ways when I talk to someone of a different race. That scares me. I also found that the topic of inter-racial dating is a touchy subject. I find that it is not really accepted down here and most people are scared—of what I'm not sure. This scares me because I guess you can say I am "mixed"; a product of an inter-racial marriage. So when I hear people say such negative things about interracial dating it upsets me. It hurts to know that people can't accept that or accept me for who I am. It hurts to stand back and listen, and unfortunately, most of the time, I am too afraid to speak my mind in fear of rejection.*

Yvonne's mother was a Bahamian of African descent and her father was American of British descent. Yvonne's long brown hair and laid-back retro dress did not allow her to be easily stereotyped. She knew that she did not look out of place on campus and, although quiet in class, she listened carefully and studied hard. She was well accepted in her residence hall and easily made friends, both black and white. What "shocked" her so forcefully was a simple comment by one of the guys in her residence hall.

Their hall had been invited to a party sponsored by one of the fraternities on campus and he said she shouldn't bring all of her friends. "The fraternity won't be very hospitable to your black friend," he warned.

Name _____ Date _____

CASE ANALYSIS WORKSHEET

Color Lines

What is this case about? Immerse yourself in this case by imagining yourself in Yvonne Richards' position and hearing someone tell you not to bring your black friend to the fraternity party.

Get the facts. List the facts that you know about Yvonne and her situation:

1. _____
2. _____
3. _____
4. _____
5. _____

State the problem, issue or question that needs to be resolved.

_____

_____

List several ways that the problem might be resolved.

1. _____
2. _____
3. _____

Write down the best way to solve the problem and why you would solve it that way.

_____

_____

_____

_____

DIVERSITY

CASE STUDY

Southern Hospitality

(This case study was prepared in cooperation with Kate Zaner Williams, Director of Experiential Education at Oglethorpe University and Corbin Smythe, Director of Co-Curricular Programs at the University of Indianapolis. It is intended solely to initiate class discussion. All names and some peripheral facts have been disguised.)

Dana Parker sat in her University 101 freshman orientation class biting her tongue. The class discussion about diversity put her at odds with many others in the class. "Why can't they just open their minds?" Dana thought.

Going South

Coming to Independence College from Massachusetts proved to be a challenge, but one that Dana had welcomed. She was always interested in learning about other people and their cultures. She saw the chance to attend college in the South as a great opportunity to do just that. Dana also looked forward to the warmer climate and being far away from home. Many of her friends stayed near home. Dana had her own style and always seemed to be one step ahead of her peers and wanted to try something new and exciting.

In some ways Independence was not exactly what Dana expected. People were not really as hospitable as she had anticipated (she had heard much about "southern hospitality"), and it was a challenge for her to make friends. Dana got to know her roommate and several other people in her residence hall, but found it difficult to branch out and meet others. It was especially hard to meet people who shared her values and interests. She started to go through Greek rush and then dropped out after the first day, but later felt like maybe she should have given it more consideration. The only activity she got involved with was her part-time job off campus as a tutor for kids in an orphanage.

Racism

Dana was surprised to find so much tolerance of racism and oppression at college. Growing up near Boston, she was exposed to many different races, and her community fought against racist attitudes. For someone to date outside of their race, or to openly accept homosexuals were norms with which she was raised. This upbringing helped her learn to acknowledge and evaluate differing opinions. She just wasn't getting that same feeling from the people around her.

An Uncomfortable Feeling

Dana thought that if she could talk to her mom about her feelings, maybe things would be better. Her mom, a social worker, always taught Dana to accept others and not to give up. But even her relationship with her mother was not as strong as it used to be before she left for college. Both her older brother and sister were still near home and Dana felt like her mom was trying to make her feel guilty. Mike, her boyfriend, was the one person that she could depend upon, but he was back in Massachusetts. She did not want to transfer up north just to be with him, but it would be nice to be a little closer to home. Now, sitting in 101, Dana wondered if she could really be happy at Independence College. There were so many differences between the north and the south. Dana found herself asking, "Will I ever find people I really click with?"

Name _____ Date _____

CASE ANALYSIS WORKSHEET

Southern Hospitality

What is this case about? Place yourself in Dana Parker's position and experience the feeling of being surrounded by people who do not share your values. How can you adjust?

Get the facts. List the facts that you know about Dana and her situation:

1. _____
2. _____
3. _____
4. _____
5. _____

State the problem, issue or question that needs to be resolved.

_____
_____

List several ways that the problem might be resolved.

1. _____
2. _____
3. _____

Write down the best way to solve the problem and why you would solve it that way.

_____
_____
_____
_____

VINCENNES UNIVERSITY LIBRARY